NINA DUNN

# STANDING BY

A walk through London's dark theatres in the time of pandemic

ISBN: 978-1-5272-7122-7
Imprint: Book Printing UK
First published by The Fifth Estate 2020
© Nina Dunn & The Fifth Estate

EDITED BY SARAH RUSHTON-READ    FOREWORD BY BONNIE LANGFORD

# Contents

> "The photos and stories in this book capture the serenity and the ghostly qualities of a world quickly left suspended and placed on hold."

# Foreword

Bonnie Langford

I wonder what they're thinking? The ghosts, I mean. And the mice, probably. I wonder if they miss us? I know I miss them, a lot.

When a performance is over for the evening and everything is switched off and tidied away, the backstage crew usually place a light on stage, 'for safety', so tradition says. It's not just any old lamp, it's called a ghost light and it features heavily in a scene at the end of the musical *Gypsy* and again in the musical *42nd Street*. I've appeared in both of those shows - they're very dear to my heart - and those scenes evoke the magic that lingers on stage when the audience has gone, yet the echoes of laughter, tears and applause still ring in the air and in the shadows of the ghost light.

The photos and stories in this book capture the serenity and the ghostly qualities of a world quickly left suspended and placed on hold.

You could be forgiven for thinking that putting on a show night after night might become monotonous and, at times, that may be true! But there's a unique energy about live theatre. It's always alive, happening instantly, in the moment and each person contributes to that moment, not only on stage and backstage, but in the box office, front of house, production and above all, in the audience.

The photos in this book reveal an almost underground community, living in the shadows and darkness. Discarded scripts nibbled by mice, props waiting to be moved, dusty lighting desks and empty dressing rooms. They are haunting, yet beautiful.

The stories reflect how events unfolded on the day in March 2020 when the pandemic meant that all the theatres closed and how we all left with unfinished business. The shows did not go on that night or since. It's an unwritten rule that a show goes on no matter what: it's the absolute last resort to cancel a performance. There's always a sense of failure in surrender, but this decision was out of everyone's hands.

It takes a large team to create and maintain a show, many people with many talents who all come together to create a product but that product is constantly evolving, growing, living. It's fascinating to discover that there's such a powerful connection within all the departments, all the roles. We all love the job. Well, it's not just a job: it's a calling, a profession, a community and on reading these accounts, it's very apparent that we all miss it.

The fabric of the buildings holds a multitude of secrets and the walls hold a wisdom, like old oak trees. They can't truly be silenced, just quietened until it's time to raise the curtain again. I, for one, cannot wait to be back in a theatre to hear the stage manager say, "Act One Beginners to the stage, please."

Until then, while there are stories to tell; creative minds to create and imagine the often unimaginable; while there are actors, singers, dancers, musicians and producers to bring it all together and, most importantly, audiences to entertain, delight and thrill, theatre will never die.

Theatre is the heartbeat of London's West End and the pandemic created a unique pause to the energy and excitement of live entertainment. In these beautifully captured moments, we can truly see beneath the surface of our spectacular theatres and appreciate how they are strangely and serenely just waiting for the lights to be switched on again.

For the community of theatre
makers waiting in the wings.

In theatre parlance, 'dark' is a term used to describe a building that has no shows running. These periods of 'darkness' are usually a temporary hiatus between shows. However, at the time of writing, the doors of every theatre in the UK and the majority of theatres globally have been closed for more than three months with no sign of opening any time soon. These are truly dark times.

"This book captures a moment in time: **a moment in history.**"

Theatres have never witnessed such widespread global closures. They remained open during the First World War and to a great extent, the Second World War. In fact, during the past century, they have only seen blanket closures during the 1918-1920 Spanish flu pandemic, when London theatres suffered extended and prolonged closures.

It is this darkness that has provided the inspiration for this book and through this endeavour, I have found a great deal of warmth and light from the spaces and the community who once inhabited them. I hope that through the photographs and testimonials in this book, you can come to know them better too.

Thanks to ATG for facilitating the project in every way possible and to all the people I interviewed. Thanks also to those who have contributed images and to everyone who has donated to the charities by purchasing this book or photographic prints. I am grateful to Sarah Rushton-Read for her constant counsel and to her team at The Fifth Estate for flying with the project and to Simon Hargreaves for creating the beautiful design. Finally, thanks to my family for their support at home, to Mary, who we have lost and who we miss dearly and for my extended theatre family, dispersed across the globe but waiting to be reunited to tell the next story. - Nina Dunn

# A walk through iconic London theatres, shuttered for three months.

# Introduction

Nina Dunn

My greatest hope for this book is that you are reading these words from a future where our theatres have flung their doors open to audiences once again and this sector is thriving like it once did.

I am writing to you, however, from a time when this future is in grave jeopardy. It's been three months since the doors of our theatres were closed in an attempt to stem the spread of the Coronavirus pandemic and since then, there has been little or no support for these institutions that are at the heart of all of our communities and which provide hundreds of thousands of jobs across the UK.

These majestic buildings have been home to some of our proudest achievements in UK arts. Theatre, as an institution, has been in existence for thousands of years and I have no doubt that it will prevail. Storytelling is at the heart of what human beings do and the ingenuity and creativity of the theatre community itself is the key to its survival. By nature we are proactive, we are creative, we are problem-solvers.

I have worked in the theatre for more than twelve years. When the theatres closed, I joined many other people who belong to this industry in trying to comprehend what this interval would mean. Being the first to close, we knew that we would be the last to open. There was a period of grieving and mourning combined with frenetic activity that seemed to go nowhere. People eventually settled in to their temporary 'new normal' and we, as makers and storytellers, started to make and tell stories once again. These stories were the green shoots of healing. We were coming to life again.

As part of this process, I too started to make again; not in the same way as before but in a new way that sought to express the situation I found myself in. I started to wonder what these theatres were like inside; what their story was, having been deserted so suddenly and for so long. I recall fending off mice as I approached my production desk for the morning's technical rehearsal session in more than one West End theatre and I imagined these mice now ruling the place in the absence of the building's usual inhabitants. Perhaps this rule had been short-lived and - starved of titbits left by visitors - they had already met their demise.

I approached The Ambassador Theatre Group - with whom I had a working relationship - to request access to the theatres to photograph them. To my delight, they granted me permission. So on a single day in June, I visited The Savoy, where *9 to 5: The Musical* had closed behind closed doors; The Playhouse Theatre where *The Seagull* would never reach its press night opening; The Ambassadors where *Kunene and the King's* run had been curtailed and the theatre stripped bare ready for the next show and The Duke of York's where *Blithe Spirit* was into the swing of a regular show run, having celebrated the press opening just a week earlier.

I didn't know what would be waiting behind these closed doors, which was thrilling. What I didn't expect was to find the theatres so patiently waiting. The epic beauty of these places can sometimes only be appreciated in their emptiness. Whether the theatre had its lights on - as in the case of the Savoy - or whether they were extinguished like in the Duke of York's, they all spoke to me in their own unique way. Silence took on a new meaning. Knowing that there was nobody anywhere nearby with the ability to turn the lights on made the darkness even more thick and impenetrable. Any written signs or text seemed to take on a new meaning. What they needed more than anything was for the people to return.

I felt compelled not only to capture the emptiness but also to tell the stories of the people who used to inhabit these buildings and to whom this book and the funds raised by sales are dedicated. Because we, the theatre makers, are the people who will bring these theatres back to life again. We will not let our stories remain untold. We are the storytellers and we will continue.

# Andrew Hilton

**Musical Director** | *9 to 5: The Musical* | The Savoy Theatre, London

When we left that day, we were totally convinced we'd go back for the last five weeks maybe, and we'd have the new cast go in. I mean, all my stuff is there — my laptop's there, my suit, my clothes — because I was utterly convinced it would be a month and then...

The first time I saw this image it really hit me. I just thought "God, that's so sad!" Although, it looks very clean: I thought it would look like Miss Havisham's place. I think it's sadder because we're now not going back.

We were all watching the news backstage throughout that last day and because Broadway had closed a few days before, it felt imminent, but I didn't ever think it would be this... permanent. We didn't get confirmation until about quarter to seven, so we were all doing warm-up. People were saying, "Do we put pin curls in?" and Bonnie [Langford] was stretching her legs. The audience arrived at half past six so we could hear the bustle in the bars and we were thinking "do we do one more show?". They must have been so disappointed after looking forward to it for months, getting babysitters in; maybe they had been out to dinner too. When we left, we all headed to the pub. It was surreal. It felt a bit naughty — like when school closes because of the snow. ☞

**The Musical Director's seat**

The orchestra pit at the Savoy Theatre

"The audience arrived at half past six so we could hear the bustle in the bars and we were thinking 'do we do one more show?'"

"It was inconceivable that it would be longer than a month and the fact that *9 to 5* didn't even reopen before it closed – we couldn't even grasp that as a concept."

## The safety curtain
The Savoy Theatre

It was inconceivable that it would be longer than a month and the fact that *9 to 5* didn't even reopen before it closed – we couldn't even grasp that as a concept. Now people are saying it could be February 2021, and that seems normal. For the group of people I work with, we've lost nine tours, six pantos and two West End shows and only three of them have mentioned coming back next year. If the shows all decide to open in January we're in trouble: we can't be in six different places at once.

During the first few months I was thinking that this was a once-in-a-lifetime forced holiday: press Ctrl+alt+del and reset because we all work too hard! I just took this opportunity to walk the dog for an hour, two hours a day and sit in the garden. I've got a brilliant housemate and on a random Wednesday we'd sit in the garden and have cocktails at two in the afternoon. Of course, it coincided with Bank Holidays and Easter – but that holiday feeling has worn off now. I was walking through Bromley the other day and it was like an apocalypse. All the shops still have Mother's Day and Easter displays. You're so used to that changing overnight. When I see a *9 to 5* poster I just feel heartbroken. They should all be gone by now.

I'm not worried about going back into the theatre because I believe I've had the virus, but I would have to do some research to find out if I can still carry it because then I would feel worse about it. The distancing thing does bother me because I love comedy and humour and I think you wouldn't laugh or enjoy something as much if you are one of 400 people spread over three levels in a venue that holds 1,200 or so. Flights I'm more worried about, because you're just breathing that recycled air for three hours or so. I hope that if people go back to pubs and bars in a week or so when they reopen, that by September they will be ready to go to the theatre. I just hope people aren't too scared to let go, to sit and enjoy it – to lose themselves in it like they used to." ●

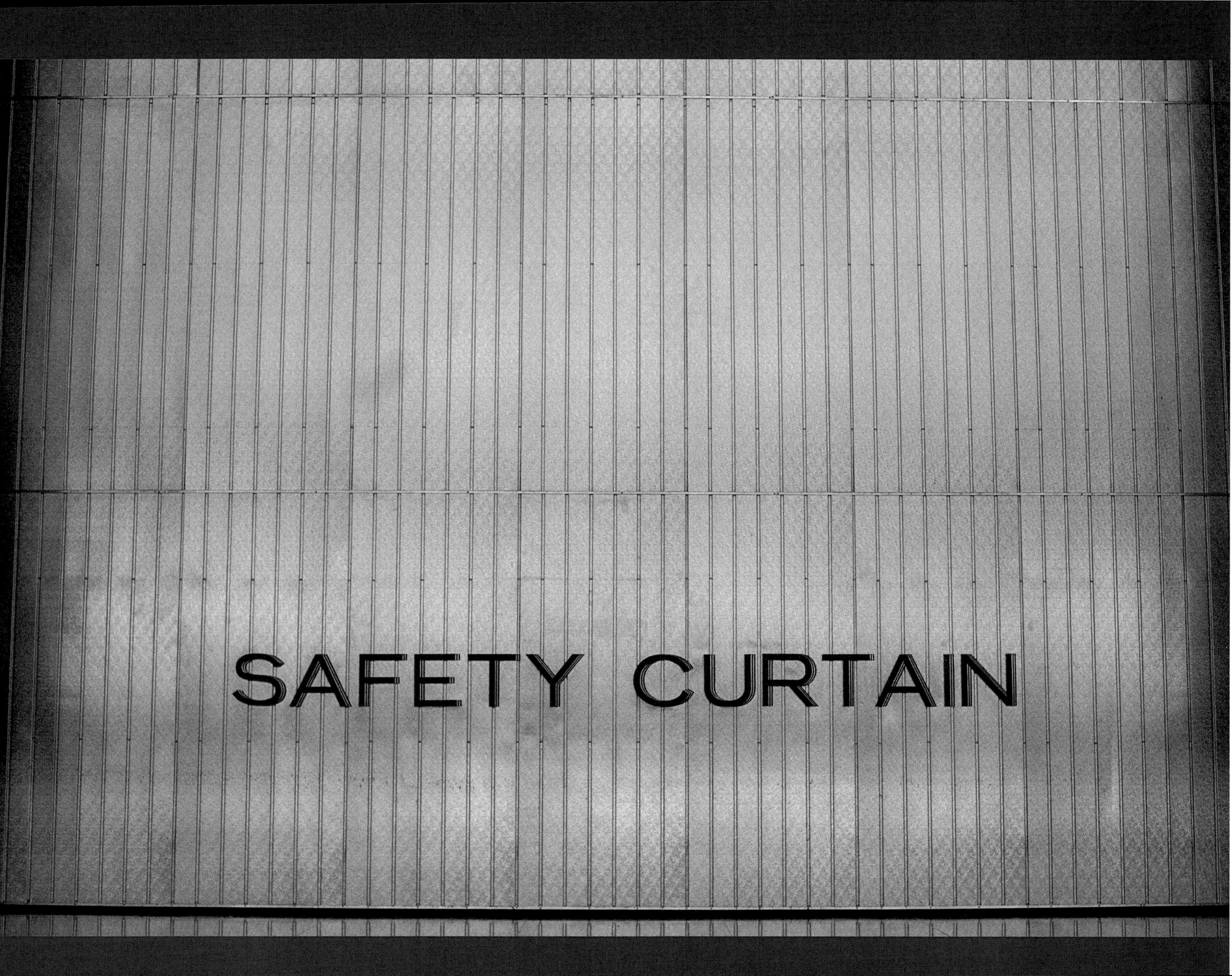
SAFETY CURTAIN

# Waiting majestically.

KUNENE AND THE KING

BY

JOHN KANI

First Rehearsal Room Draft, 20/01/2023

# 02

# Andy John Evans

Head of Sound | *Kunene and the King* | The Ambassadors Theatre, London

I'm back at home in Llanelli, South Wales, with my parents and I'm relaxing into it for now. I did have to leave the London flat: I was one day away from signing a new tenancy agreement. I had already received my next work contract but had started to feel like the coronavirus was gaining ground and was going to impact us sooner than we thought. I phoned Regent's Park and asked if they thought the season was going to go ahead. It was a nervous answer, understandably.

A friend and I had decided to treat ourselves and get a really nice flat for once and live a little 'high' life for a while. I mean why not? Sixteen years working and living in run-of-the-mill London accommodation. But without a guarantee that the season would go ahead, I couldn't sign the agreement then risk around seven months of work being wiped out. It was a lucky escape, because the season was later cancelled. At the end of April I managed to get a six-month contract working for the NHS at my local hospital. The contract takes me to the end of October. I was thinking I would finish in time for the Christmas season, but that's not looking great at the moment either, unfortunately.

> "I sometimes think about what the theatres are like inside without the people. How quickly does a theatre become uninhabitable?"

There was a murmur the week before [the theatres closed] among the company - the virus was starting to become something that they were beginning to be more concerned about. Our two main cast members were elderly actors from South Africa and with the rumour that there was going to be a lockdown, the company manager was worried about flights getting cancelled and them not being able to get back to their family and homes. They were also really vulnerable to the virus.

On the Monday, everything was sort of as normal until about 6pm when the company manger came down and said that although she hadn't heard anything official, the Front of House Manager had told her they had information that the whole of the West End was going to get shut down that night. Until she received something solid she couldn't action that, so she called us all to the stage to inform us of what she knew. Just before the doors were due to open, we were told that we were going to have to cancel the show. We were planning on coming in again the next day as normal but, two hours later, once more information had started to come through, the producers stated that the rest of our run was to be cancelled. Ten minutes later the news came that every performance in the West End was cancelled that evening - and would likely not perform again anytime soon, either.

There was a moment of reflection on stage and a weird silence for a little while as the scale of what was happening settled in. Obviously we went straight to the pub, The Two Princes, for a pint. By the time we got there, the *City of Angels* band were already there and then *The Mousetrap* cast came in and our team from *Kunene* were there too. That in itself was surreal: during audience walk-in time we were in a pub! It was actually really sad, because it felt like there was a bit of a storm over us. There were people visibly upset because the *Mousetrap* cast were really close to the end of their six-month contract and the feeling was, that was that. There were musicians with their guitars and keyboards and I think they knew immediately it wasn't going to be just a week or two: it was going to be a long haul and they could maybe teach online.

Because the guys behind the bar knew who we all were (regular regulars), they let us pour our own pints for a while, so that was really fun. A lot of people had a couple of drinks but were feeling melancholy. Some people were worried about their immediate future, financially especially. At this early stage there had been no support announcements (although a fair few of us have fallen through that support system now anyway). I could see it in their faces and their eyes - they wanted to go home and gather their thoughts. It's a lot of information to take on board and process suddenly. You start thinking about the next six months straight away: what if there isn't any work? Am I going to be financially okay? Are my kids going to be supported? It was a very peculiar and overwhelming evening. We were together and talking and trying to offer advice and support for going forward in differing scenarios. I must have spoken to a dozen people that evening in depth about what had just happened. It was comforting that we were all in the same boat and could relate and respond to concerns.

## Stage door
The Ambassadors Theatre

There was a feeling that London was going to be the first city into total lockdown and that we might not be able to travel. At kicking out time it was really strange: the streets were quiet and we knew that this was way more serious than we had thought. It felt like an apocalypse: the invisible war... which is what it is really. The place was usually littered with audience members pouring out and getting in the way of us reaching tube stations. That night there was nothing. Silence, an eerie silence: like a ghost town.

I sometimes think about what the theatres are like inside without the people. How quickly does a theatre become uninhabitable? It's only been three months but it's going to be longer - nine months, maybe a year for some theatres - so how much will it then cost to get it back to a state where you can use it again? The Ambassadors is riddled with mice and they're brave. I was putting someone's mic on one day and a mouse popped up and started eating the grapes on the table. They've gone from only coming out at night to wandering around in full light. They must be having a party right now!

When you think about a pandemic, we are not classed as essential by the government. But it is essential to all of us who are working in the industry. I knew that, along with pubs and gyms, we would be the first to go and we'd be the last to be back. That was quite a worrying thought. I felt it would be a long time. The worry is, we aren't seeing anything for us on the news or from Boris about the Arts. I've not once heard anyone talking about the creative industries and what help can be given to them financially, or when they think large gatherings might be okay again. No guidelines as to what social distancing measures will ☞

> "We'll find a way: we still need to keep hoping and fighting and get our voices heard, but I know a lot of my friends are having a really hard time at the moment. We may be past the peak, but we're still in mid-air and the uncertainty is what is causing the anxiety and it's not going to go away."

**Locked foyer doors**
The Ambassadors Theatre

need to be in place so venues can start to judge whether it's financially viable for them to open, nor any offers of support from the government in doing that. It's more difficult to be optimistic when the people running your country aren't giving you anything to hope for. When the furlough starts tapering, who knows what will happen?

I'm determined that there will be a way. It may not be perfect, but just something. We all love this industry and we've all been in it since an early age and for it to be in such jeopardy and to have nobody at the top talking about it or how they might support it, it's heartbreaking. You think 'it can't happen; we'll get bailed out', but not at the moment. Theatres and venues are closing up and down the country already. This week, producers have started to put redundancy packages together, which means they will have to go through the whole process of re-hiring, with interviews and auditions etc. Cameron Mackintosh are making decisions and putting hundreds of redundancy packages together and that means for those who are affected, everything is in jeopardy - their mortgage, way of life, childcare etc. That's such a massive thing to happen in someone's life. I do question producers' motives for staying closed and not wanting to adapt the venues for social distancing measures, especially the larger producers. It's their job to look at numbers.

I've been thinking a lot about how we work when we do go back. The main thing is that everybody feels safe - safe enough to do their jobs. Trying to adapt venues would cost a lot of money, money they really don't have, especially considering how much has been lost of late. There will need to be changes in seating; hand sanitiser everywhere; new rules for the toilets; more staff. But

I also applaud innovation and motivation. As an industry, we're a really close-knit group and even though we might not see each other regularly, there are a lot of amazing brains and passionate people out there. I wouldn't go back just yet though. It's more to do with protecting vulnerable people. There are a lot of people I care about - family and friends - who are vulnerable. Because we're still in the midst of it, I wouldn't want to be in an environment that could re-ignite infection. As much as I love this industry, everyone's health is more important.

We'll find a way: we still need to keep hoping and fighting and get our voices heard, but I know a lot of my friends are having a really hard time at the moment. We may be past the peak, but we're still in mid-air and the uncertainty is causing anxiety and it's not going to go away. I just hope that those people have had the right support through this. I also hope that people who struggle with their mental health are doing as well as they can be. I often suffer from anxiety, and I've had some really tough days. This time, more than ever, can induce a lot of worry and anxiety and I hope everyone's head space is keeping as healthy as can be through this turbulent time.

We just seem to be unimportant to the Government. What do we do? Do we protest? We need to stand together and try to use the voices among us, whether it's as a collective or as individuals. We need to use the biggest voices in our Industry - the Dame Judy Denches of this world - to do as Marcus Rashford did: he managed to overturn a government policy within 24 hours. This has rocked our industry to the core, the pandemic and now the lack of support after it. It needs attention, and fast. ●

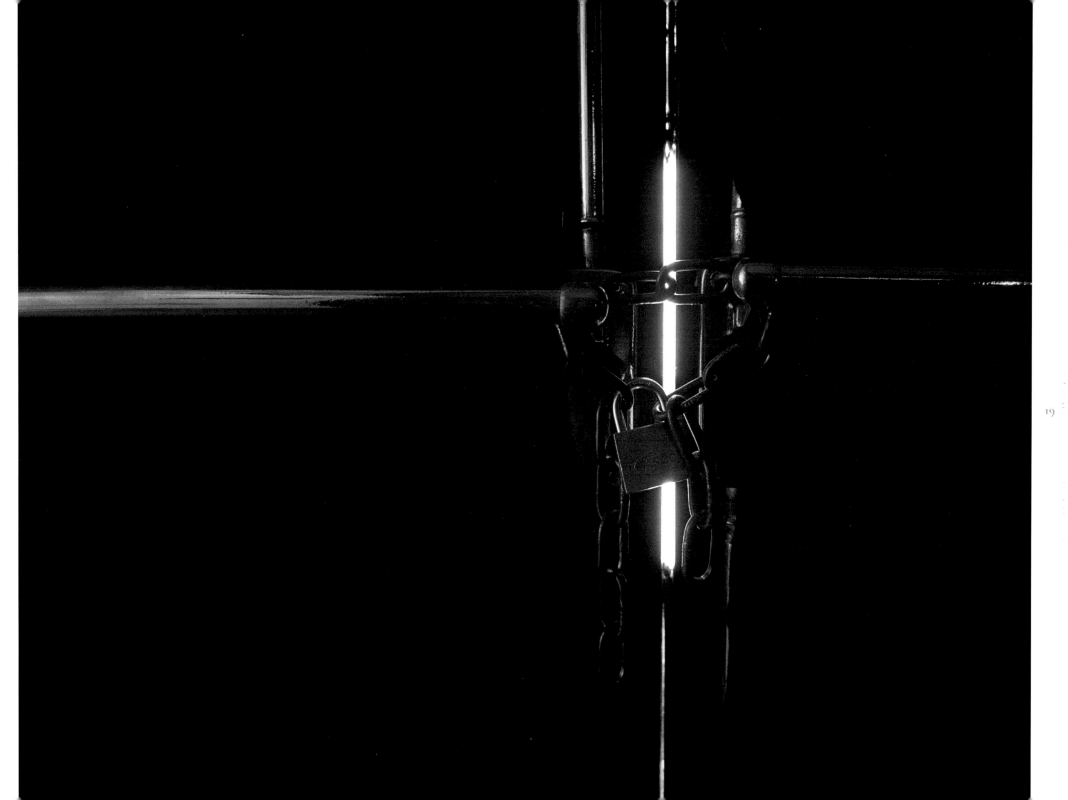

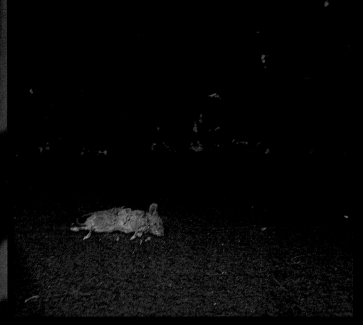

Decay.

NEWSPAPER CUP & SAUCER

03

# Sarah Myott-Meadows

**Associate Director** | *Blithe Spirit* | **Duke of York's Theatre, London**

I was associate director on *Blithe Spirit* during its initial run at the Theatre Royal Bath and its subsequent tour and West End transfer. I was responsible for running rehearsals with Richard Eyre and rehearsing the understudies. The show has some mildly technical elements such as flying and an intricately-timed final sequence including some magic tricks, so perfecting this was also a part of my role. Once the show was up, my daily/weekly responsibilities involved show watches and notes with the main cast and weekly on-stage understudy rehearsals. I would also be there to support stage management or the main cast in any ongoing technical issues or changes needed once the production was running and we understood its demands. I was also opening my own show, *One Jewish Boy,* at Trafalgar Studios, so was sharing my time between both productions in The West End.

I remember two days before the theatres officially shut, I went to watch a matinée - with a predominantly older audience - of *One Jewish Boy* at Trafalgar Studios and felt very uncomfortable and by that point I was willing the industry to make the decision itself, despite woolly government guidelines. I could feel things changing in that moment and knew how big this was going to be in the history of the theatre industry. ☞

**A very long interval**
The Duke of York's Theatre

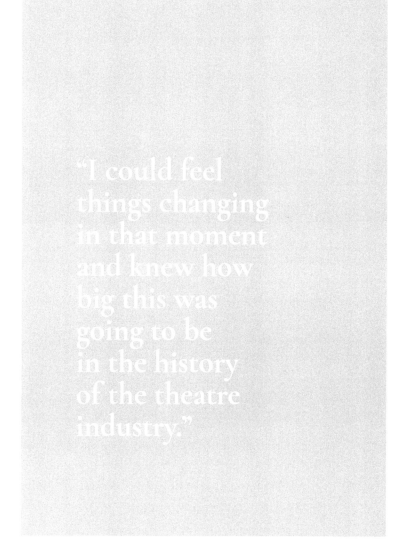

"I could feel things changing in that moment and knew how big this was going to be in the history of the theatre industry."

On the day the theatres shut down, the directive came just as stage management were beginning to prepare for the show. I was not due to do a show watch at *Blithe Spirit* and my assistant director attended *One Jewish Boy,* so I wasn't in town, but I remember being sent pictures from both casts as the entire West End descended on the local pubs for one last drink.

The actors said they sat and drank with the cast of *Waitress* amongst others and there was a very strange, 'last supper' feel in the air while they all imagined what was to be faced ahead. I was at home with my then seven-month-old baby and was feeling the loss of my two West End shows that had just opened. There was also the fear of what was to come and questions of how we will survive this.

I hope this provides us with a chance to rethink how we work and connect with new audiences properly, making theatres the civic spaces they should be and inspiring collaboration between buildings and freelancers on how we make shows, as we will have to make them differently now. I hope that shows considered a 'risk' will now be seen as work that needs to be put on. It is no coincidence that we are witnessing a civil rights movement at the same time as this pandemic. It is all entwined and theatres, more than ever, need to progressively reflect these changes. Society has changed and theatre must be a leader for society. ●

"I hope this provides us with a chance to rethink how we work and connect with new audiences … Society has changed and theatre must be a leader for society."

**Behind the curtain**
The Duke of York's Theatre

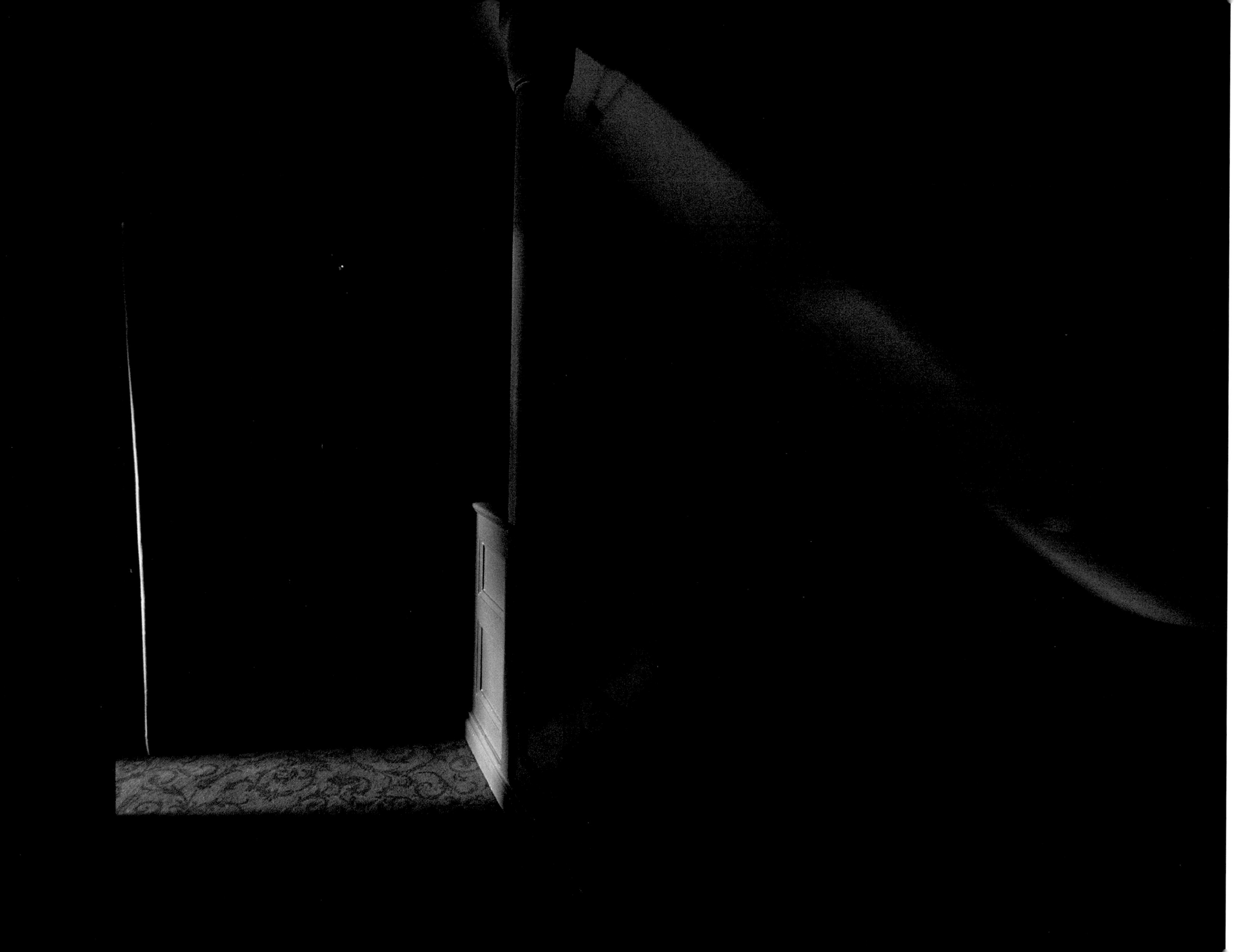

# 04

# Natalie McQueen

**Performer** | *9 to 5: The Musical* | The Savoy Theatre, London

We were actually on stage warming up for the show that evening. We all knew something was happening so a few people had their phones and were watching the news of other shows and theatres announcing they wouldn't be performing that evening. As we finished warm-up, we were told the news.

We kind of knew it would happen at some point. For me personally, and a few others in the cast, we were actually finishing our contracts around two weeks later, so there was a real gutting feeling knowing we may never perform *9 to 5* again. Unfortunately, that did happen, for all of the cast sadly. We had no idea at the time how long it would be, but I had a feeling I wouldn't finish up my run as Doralee.

It's the weirdest feeling knowing that a whole part of my life exists in a space I haven't seen in months. Also, that room was ready for a show that evening. There's probably lash glue on a lash ready to go for that night. Going back to collect everything will be a really surreal moment I'm sure.

Would I go back to the theatre right now? It's a tough one because, obviously people want to return to theatres to be entertained and I'm sure socially distanced seating is a real possibility, but the fact is, that side may be a lot simpler than what would be able to happen on stage. On and off stage we are in such close contact. I of course miss theatre, but safety is the most important thing here.

I truly cannot wait to get back in to the audition room and back onto a stage. Once I've cleared up my Savoy dressing room first, of course! ●

> "It's the weirdest feeling knowing that a whole part of my life exists in a space I haven't seen in months. There's probably lash glue on a lash ready to go for that night."

**Dressing room**
The Savoy Theatre

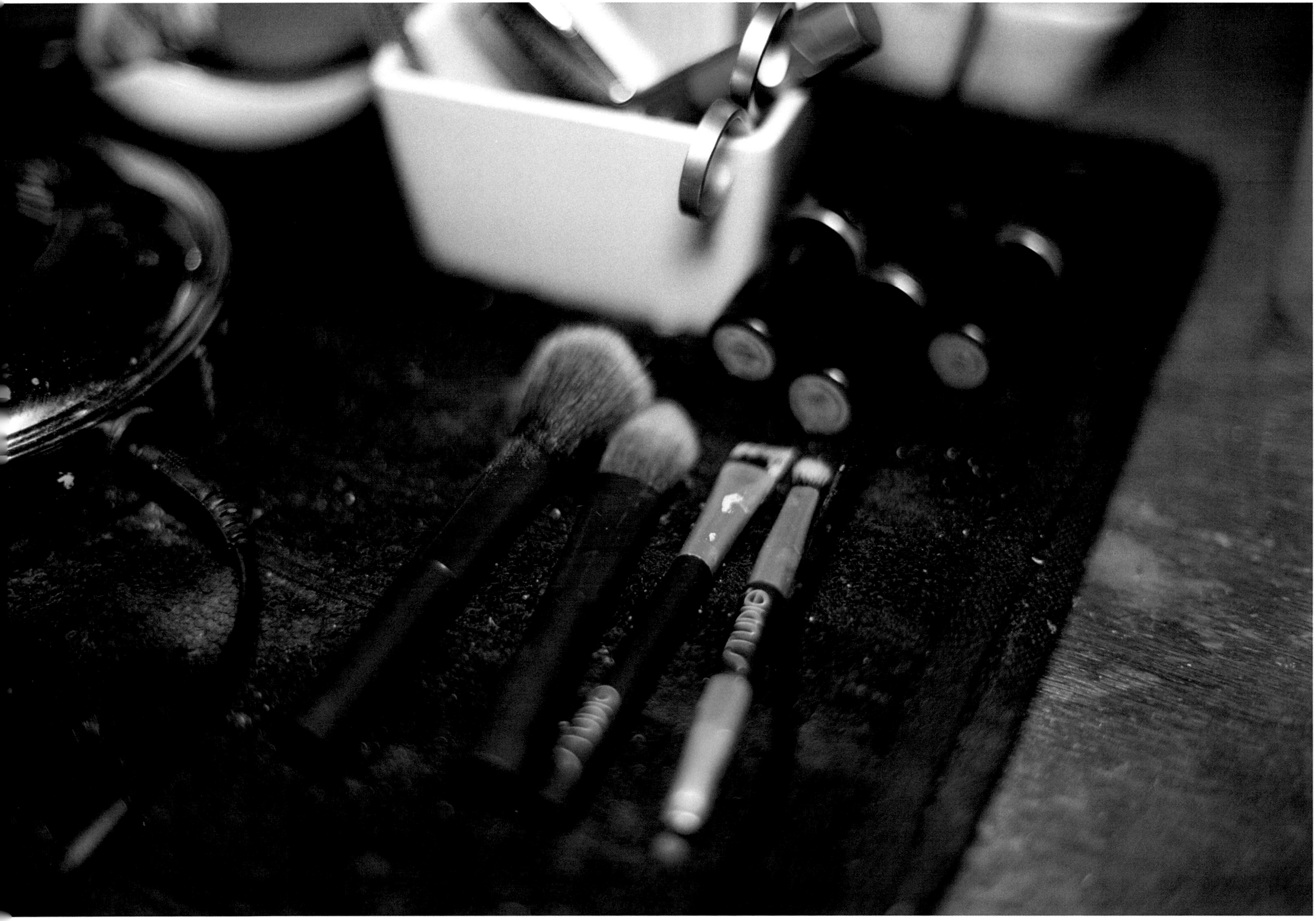

Standing by.

> "I just remember watching Boris when he first said that immortal phrase along the lines of 'Don't go to the theatre but we're not going to tell them to close'."

**The empty auditorium**
The Ambassadors Theatre

# 05

# Andreas Ayling

**Production Manager** | *Kunene and the King* | The Ambassadors Theatre, London

I just remember watching Boris when he first said that immortal phrase along the lines of "Don't go to the theatre, but we're not going to tell them to close." My phone went off – it was my colleague from The Ambassadors – and we had a very nothing conversation where we just said, "What are we going to do?"

That day, both Anthony [Sher] and John [Kani] were going to be off anyhow and as bizarre as it felt, we said, "We'll just close the show". We only had two weeks of the run left and both Tony and John were in the high-risk category, so it just seemed the most pragmatic decision. There could have been some grounds to do it with the understudies, but the show was selling on John, who had also written the play, and Tony. Such a beautiful and poignant piece, especially considering the Black Lives Matter protests and the way in which people of colour are seen.

Once we knew the show was closing it was a question of whether we could get staff in to buildings and we had to find out what the deal was with all the hire companies. One said they had no space because everything was closing, so we could keep it if we wanted, whereas another supplier said that until Boris declared an actual lockdown they were going to potentially keep charging for the equipment rental. The theatre said we could leave everything there, but there was a question of insurance. ☞

> "Obviously, it was heartbreaking that the show was going to close early because it was a show that everyone loved ... but it was the human side of things - when you can't properly thank someone like you would normally - that really hit me afterwards."

**The empty stage and grid**
The Ambassadors Theatre

We went for the option of the full get-out, but we had to be done by 6pm because there was rumour that the lockdown was coming. During the get-out everyone was very much already trying not to shake hands or hug. It was bizarre: there were a lot of us who over such a short period of time had become close, so it was weird when we saw each other not to hug or anything like that. We had all said that when we did the get-out, I'd take them for a beer to say thank you for everything, but when we finished it was like "Well, we can't do that, so see you at some point then. All the best!".

Obviously it was heartbreaking that the show was going to close early, because it was a show that everyone loved and a wonderful show to be part of, but it was the human side of things - when you can't properly thank someone like you would normally - that really hit me afterwards. You know what they say: 'You don't do theatre for the money, you do it for the love' and that's true. I can't imagine the next time I see my colleagues that I can't give them a hug.

We don't even know when that will be.

I decided I would go and stay with my mum because she's on her own. It's great that people are able to spend more time together – families – but equally sometimes you just want to be on your own. Luckily, Troubadour had put me on a contract, so I'm on furlough and have an income, so really all I have been doing is baking, daily walks and far too many Health and Safety courses that I never thought I'd be doing, including new WHO and COVID ones. Just doing things to stop me from watching Disney or Netflix all day.

When we go back I would like to see the theatres made more accessible in terms of both the spaces and ticket prices. On a bigger scale there are certain companies that will have to look carefully at ticket prices. For a family of four to go and see a new musical, it can cost £400-£500. I completely understand why ticket prices have risen to where they are, but it's slightly worrying when you think that fifteen years ago, a top-price seat was £60, whereas now it's upwards of £120, so it would be nice to see theatre made a bit more accessible to everyone. Broadcasts allow more people to see shows, so there needs to be a bit more of that and generally more care given to the theatres themselves. The Ambassadors is one of the most inaccessible in the West End: there's no lift, there are stairs everywhere and the seats aren't that nice, so it needs a bit of love. Theatre Royal Brighton is a favourite and it's got such a lovely history, but if it wasn't for the staff I don't think anyone would tour there because it's becoming harder and harder to get a show in that won't bring the grid down! With how things are going at the moment, I think refurbishing and ticket prices are the last things that are going to change." ●

Deserted.

36

"It felt incredibly sad to be told that we needed to pack up our things and head home, but absolutely necessary in the wider context of what was happening."

**Untouched for three months**
Backstage at the Savoy Theatre

# 06

# Merlin O'Brien

**Sound Engineer** | *9 to 5: The Musical* | The Savoy Theatre, London

I was halfway through eating my reheated pasta when the call went out backstage for everyone from all departments to go down to the stage immediately. There are very few occasions when the whole company is asked to assemble on stage, and it's not normally to celebrate. Having previously worked on shows that have received their closing notice after weeks of speculation and gossip, this felt strangely familiar - the only difference being we weren't given six months, three months, or even two weeks.

It felt incredibly sad to be told that we needed to pack up our things and head home, but absolutely necessary in the wider context of what was happening. Although the news was upsetting - shocking - there were practicalities to be dealt with. We collected the radio mics that had already been dished out to dressing rooms and put batteries back on charge. We powered down the sound desk, the amps, the LED wall and the video racks.

We even finished our dinner in the dressing room and I shared a cheeky beer I found in the fridge with my deputy, Tom. We then did what anyone would do when anything vaguely stressful, sad, or indeed happy happens: we went to the pub.

For me, there was a feeling of relief when we were told that the show wouldn't be going ahead that night. In the weeks leading up to the closure, as we watched what was happening around the world as countries began to shut down, the anxiety over what would happen to us began to grow. We talked about the show closing for a short period of time no longer as an 'if' but a 'when'. It seemed strange to watch daily briefings from the government, waiting for an update on the future of mass gatherings, which intensified the seriousness of the matter that we were dealing with. BBC News doesn't normally mention a musical about to receive its closing notice.

Over the last few shows at the Savoy I had started saying – half jokingly – that I was mixing that night's show thinking that it might be my last. I mixed the final playout for the evening show on the 14th a little louder than I would normally: I wanted to enjoy it. Sadly, it did turn out to be the last time I would ever mix the show. Afterwards, I looked up to the MD monitor to see Andrew Hilton saying his goodbyes to the musicians in the pit and the full sadness of the situation hit me. Standing at the back of an auditorium of 1,200 people seemed like the wrong thing to be doing at the time, but it didn't make it any easier to accept that we wouldn't be back doing it for a very long time.

Aside from the obvious negative impacts of the closures, I hope that we see some positive changes further down the line. Sound departments are often thinly staffed and are left unable to self-cover sick leave days, relying on a pool of freelancers being available to come in and cover. At a time when people's health has been pushed to the forefront of our minds, I am hoping that this forces a conversation about how we could staff our departments more effectively, and change some of the working conditions that we have become accustomed to. I hope that in a time of enforced rules and rigidity, theatre comes out the other side as a more flexible, adaptable industry.

I have no doubt that we will find a new, safer way of returning to work. I'm sure I'm not alone in wondering how a quick-change backstage - often involving wardrobe, wigs and sound - would ever be able to happen under the current restrictions. The nature of our jobs backstage is the complete antithesis of how we are being told we need to live our lives currently. We will need to find new ways of working and we will need to change and adapt and be willing to do so. This is an opportunity to think creatively about how to achieve what is so ingrained in us and not a time to be digging our heels in because 'we always did it this way'. We might not be able to fit radio mics the way we would like to, but we have the best and brightest minds in the industry ready to come up with new methods, and maybe with time these will become the new norm. ●

**A view from the wings**
The Savoy Theatre

"I mixed the
final playout
a little louder
than I would
normally:
I wanted
to enjoy it.
Sadly it did
turn out to be
the last time
I would ever
mix the show."

Behind the scenes.

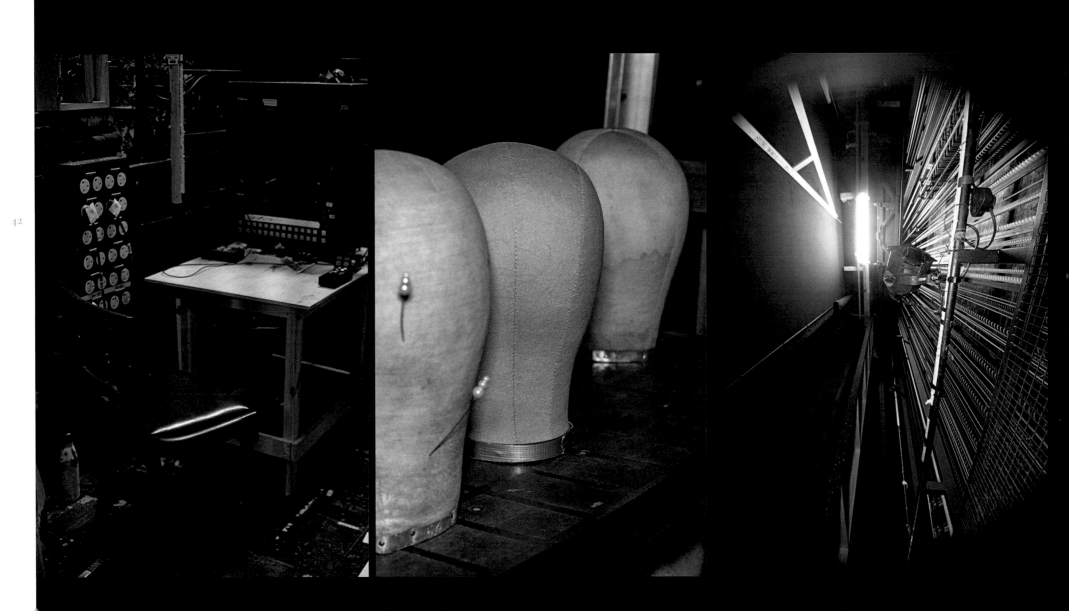

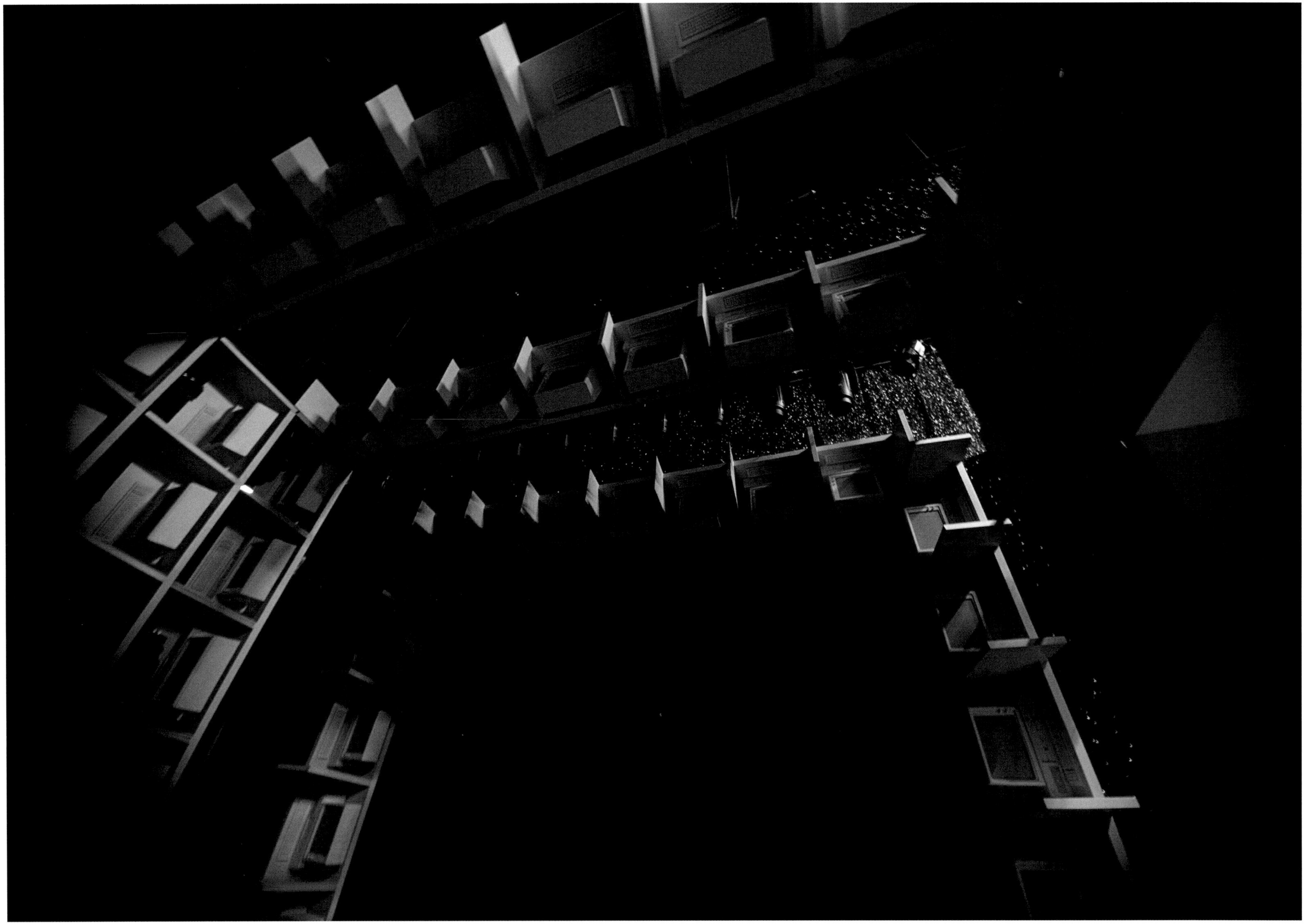

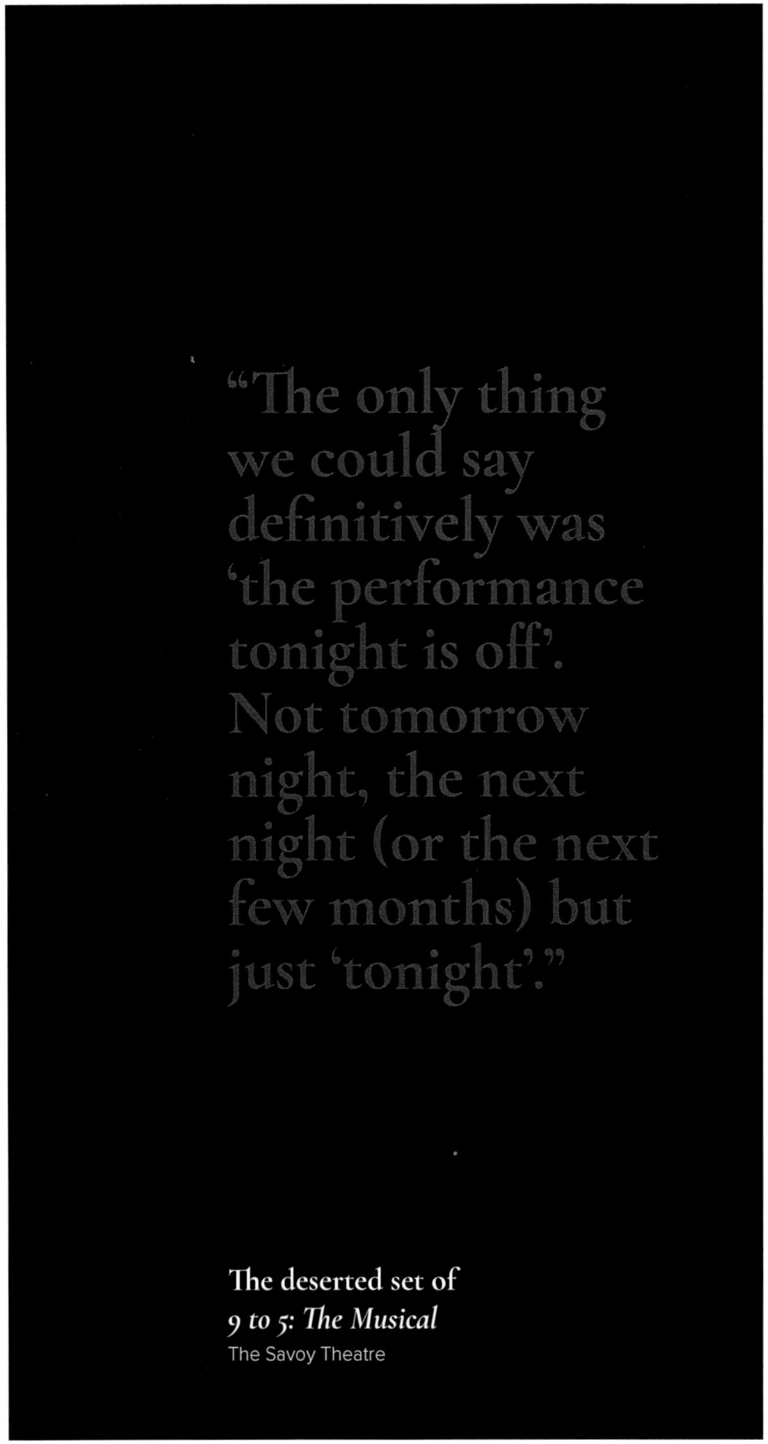

> "The only thing we could say definitively was 'the performance tonight is off'. Not tomorrow night, the next night (or the next few months) but just 'tonight'."

**The deserted set of**
*9 to 5: The Musical*
The Savoy Theatre

07

# Richard Darbourne

Producer | Ambassador Theatre Group (ATG Productions)

16th March is a day we'll never forget at ATG Productions. In terms of any shut-down we thought we might be able to see the week out and, if it came, we weren't thinking months at that point: more like weeks. At the time though, I remember feeling a sense of 'you don't know anything except the day you're in'.

On that day, we knew there was a speech coming from the Government around 5:15pm. The whole industry - actors, crews, producers and venue owners - all heard the same news in real-time as it was announced that theatres 'should' close immediately. In the follow-up questions, a journalist asked something along the lines of, "Are you telling them to shut?" and the response was that they obviously had the powers to do that, but they suspected theatres would make their own decisions. When those words were uttered, I caught the eye of Exec. Producer, Adam Speers, and we all just collectively drew breath. We knew there and then that there was nothing definitive to go on, but we had to make a decision.

It was around half past five, so we had to get moving. The only thing we could say definitively was "the performance tonight is off". Not tomorrow night, the next night (or the next few months) but just "tonight".

> ## "As a community of practitioners we are much better at action than inaction. We're having to go against all our natural instincts which are telling us to go out there and just make it work."

**The empty auditorium**
The Savoy Theatre

We had four shows running in London: two had already closed in the US and another on tour. We were all very deeply connected to the people in all of them but we couldn't all be in all places, so the three Producers in our team and our General Manager had to split up and go alone to the ones we could. I went to *Pretty Woman* at the Piccadilly where the cast and crew had been gathered. I was struck by the calm grace with which the company took the news. All the cast gathered together on stage in a very un-socially distanced group hug and said, "We'll be OK. We'll get through this" - and that was it. There was a lot of love around. They just took the statement and off they went.

I then went round to Front of House where the audience were starting to come in. The box office had learned the news and had started to turn patrons away at the door. One lady said, "Oh no, that's a shame - is the bar still open?" As it happened, it was, so a lot of people just went up to the bar!

The four of us arrived back at the office and rejoined the team. Some of our co-producers were around and there was a small gathering of other people who didn't know where to go, so they all came to our office and we ordered pizza and had a few beers. There were people there who we later learned had COVID at the time. That was the last time we physically saw all of our team of eleven in person. ATG's CEO emailed saying we were all going to work from home from that moment on, so having just closed the shows, we had to clear out of the office. It felt weighty and - dare I say it - unprecedented.

As a community of practitioners we are much better at action than inaction. That's what's hard about this particular scenario: we're having to go against all our natural instincts which are telling us to go out there and just make it work. Anyone who thrives in the theatre industry does so because they are a positive problem-solver. If we have one common thing amongst us, it's that.

Going forward, I think about our audiences and how we can welcome them back. It sounds obvious, but it's about them and not us. Audiences need to feel they have been looked after and valued, and they have had a really, really good time. If you get that right - not just with the content but the experience as a whole - then it's healthy. That needs to be at the heart of how we embrace the 'new normal'. ●

Preservation.

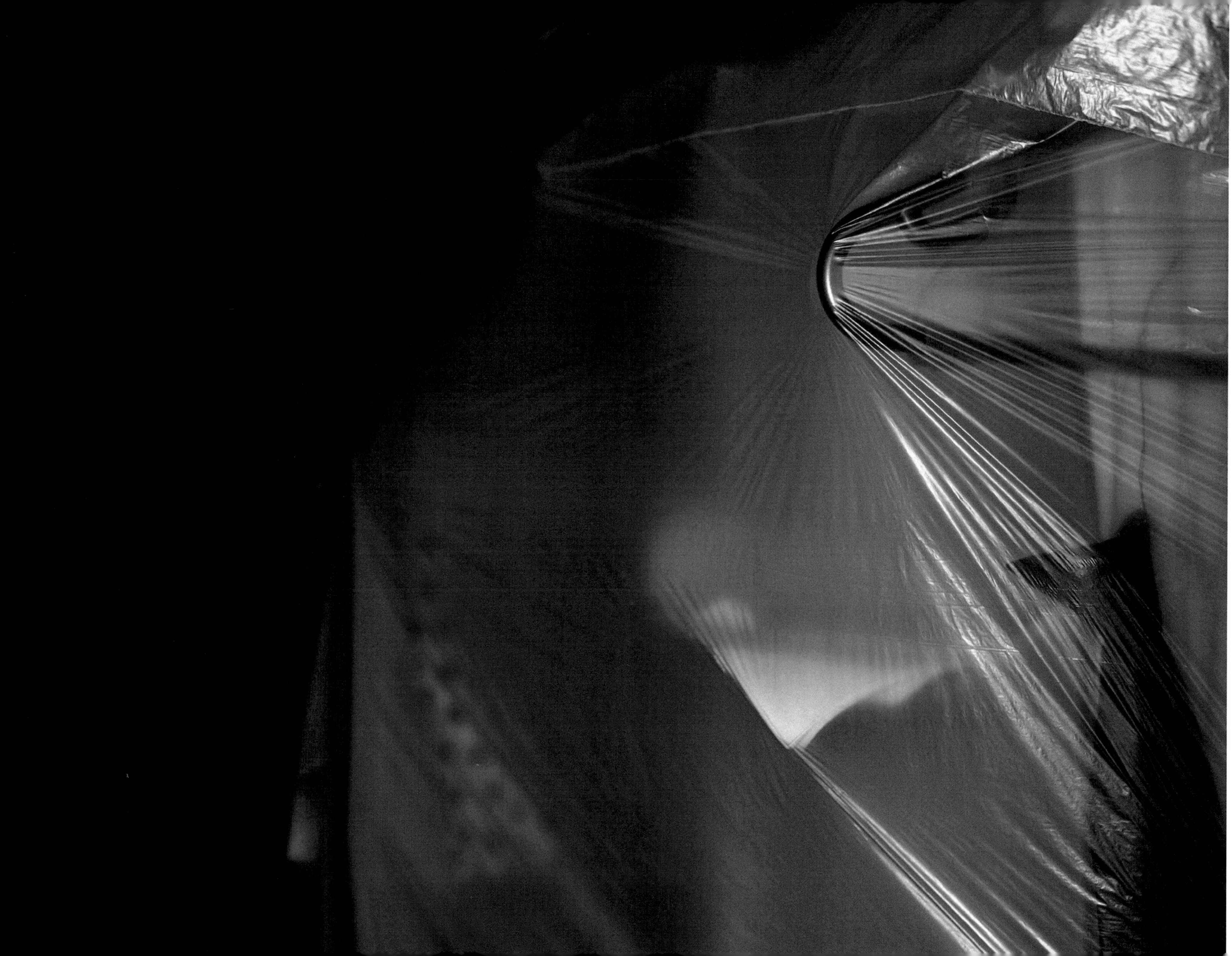

"If it were
a play, the
history of
that day
would have
a rather
anticlimactic
ending!"

**View from the upper circle**
The Duke of York's Theatre

# 08

# Howard Harrison

Lighting Designer | *Blithe Spirit* | Duke of York's Theatre, London

We had opened *Blithe Spirit* the week before, so I was actually at The Garrick working on *City of Angels,* but bizarrely I had just been for a meeting earlier in the day at the Duke of York's on the Monday we were all sent home. Believe it or not, the two theatres are actually connected: you can get from one to the other if you go up to the top floor. At one point they were sister theatres and used to share a stage door. We had done *Blithe Spirit* this time last year in Bath and it then got mothballed until January when it went out on tour in an adapted version. Then, of course, it came into town at exactly the same time we were supposed to be at the Garrick doing *City of Angels,* so I spent less time there than I would have liked to because the other show was very demanding, but I had very good associates and it all went very smoothly. I kept turning up at breaks and everybody said "What are you doing here?" so I just came back to the Garrick. For me, it was a weird thing having two shows going on back-to-back, at the same time. Two such different shows - two completely different teams with different atmospheres - it was kind of extraordinary.

Looking at the image from the circle, it makes me think that someone is about to take the iron out and it's all going to be fine. Everyone's going to be on stage and we're back to normal.

The week before, you just knew something was about to happen but it was interesting to see how everyone reacted to it that day: the various factions and disagreements about whether we should perform. We were having a conversation about it and trying to decide what to do, but then the Government broadcast came out and there was no decision to be made after all. If it were a play, the history of that day would have a rather anticlimactic ending! ☞

## Waiting in the wings
The Duke of York's Theatre

"People will
say, 'You did
the show that
never opened.'
It will become
the stuff of
legends."

52

I presume at the Duke of York's they didn't play that night either. It was a very happy show, *Blithe Spirit*. It was a lovely company, a very pleasant experience and a very good production. This backstage image sums up *Blithe Spirit* to me because it was all very naturalistic so we wanted to hide the lights from view. Jennifer [Saunders] was a very good company leader and she was incredibly good in the show - as was everyone - so it was terribly sad that it turned out to be such a short run. It was only due to be eight weeks or so and it was Sod's law that it was doing incredibly well. I presume the set's still sitting there.

Who knows, maybe it will come back again. It was supposed to close in May and there were another two shows backed up going in there - absolutely chock-a-block. I don't know what's happened to those shows - whether they will reappear. That's the thing: we just don't know. There's a big question mark hanging over all of us. Weird times indeed and one day we'll probably all go "Where were you when...?".

I think we'd all hope that when we go back, we'd want to return to an enlightened version of where we were. I think there are a lot of things about the world that will need to change. The lockdown and the virus has pointed out to us that the way the world works is not great and we could do with being aware of this and starting again. However, I think in the theatre everything was going pretty well. It was pretty healthy, everyone was going to see shows; it was good, so it would be great to think we'd go back to the way things were, but maybe we never will. Who knows?

Obviously, it was terribly sad with *City of Angels* because it was a great show and we'd all been working extremely hard on it. We'd got so far and to get that close to the finishing line was desperately unfair. We were shut down on the Monday and we were supposed to open on the following Tuesday so we were eight shows away from opening. I think there's something quite poetic about that. People will say "You did the show that never opened." It will become the stuff of legends. ●

Behind closed doors.

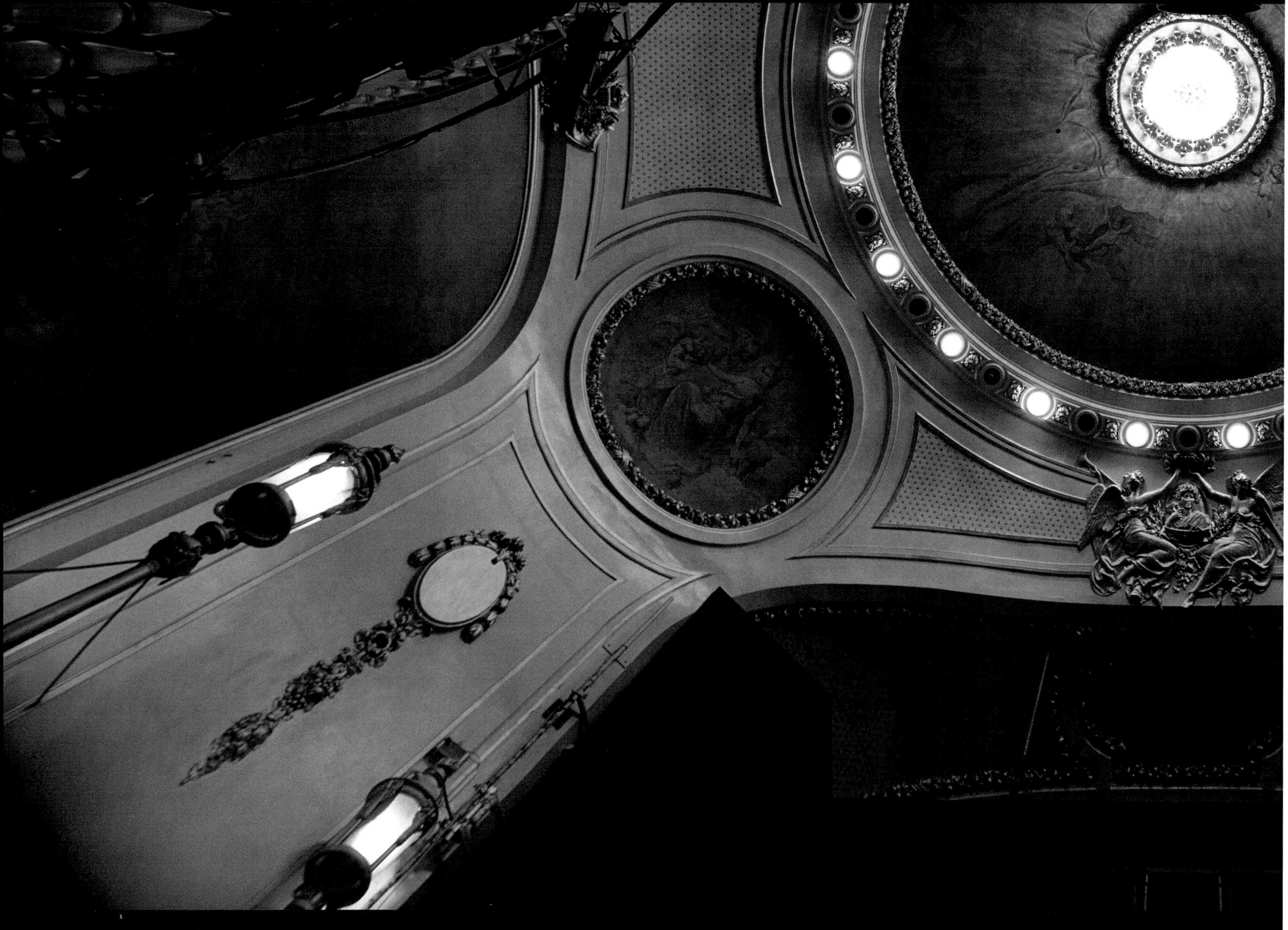

Fire
exit

Your
STAGE DOOR KEEPER
is

> "I have been trying to enjoy being with the kids, cooking dinner for the family, reading *Harry Potter*, but I do feel like there is a big chunk of my life missing and that's theatre."

**An absent stage door keeper**
Backstage - The Playhouse Theatre

# 09

# Nicolas Egen

**Company Stage Manager** | *The Seagull* | **Playhouse Theatre, London**

I've just taken over an allotment. It was hard work, quite physical to start with because I had to turn it over from being completely unused but I was finding it quite cathartic - growing things - and grateful for the physical work and the distraction. It's almost like for a while there I treated it as work, especially in those first few weeks when everyone was trying to find some sort of normality. I'd get up in the morning, get the kids ready, they would do home schooling with my wife, then I would hop over my back fence and work hours and hours. I just needed some sort of rhythm and schedule.

That feels like an eternity ago. We're now one hundred days since the start of lockdown - a week longer since the theatres closed, and it's still incredibly surreal. I am lucky enough to be in a reasonable personal situation. We're down in Brighton with the beach and the Downs and my family and that's all wonderful, but I have moments of crashing reality where I think, "This is actually happening," and they are becoming more frequent. I find as soon as the weather gets you indoors, that's where I hit the wall. Space and fresh air is everything.

What can I do? Rage? Get active? On a personal level what do I do? Do I sit here waiting? Do I apply for work that isn't out there? There are so many questions. I have tried just to relax and go with it: there is no fighting it. I had a dry period last year where I didn't work for about four weeks and now I laugh thinking about how long it's been now. I have been trying to enjoy being with the kids, cooking dinner for the family, reading *Harry Potter*, but I do feel like there is a big chunk of my life missing and that's theatre. 🖝

I started in theatre when I was fifteen. This is what I have always done. I've changed continents to do this (I'm from New Zealand). I left home when I was eighteen and worked in Australia for seven years then moved over here to follow the industry. Those are the sacrifices we make. It's always been about theatre for me, so to have it gone – to have it taken away – it leaves such a gap. Once you've accepted that theatre is your life, it's everything. Every time I look at other jobs it always comes back to theatre. I don't really want to do anything else.

Thankfully, we've been really well looked after by our management and producers. We started off with Zoom calls every week, then every two weeks, then four. It's a constant conversation about where we're at, what's being done and where we're heading. I know there is a bigger picture and we get lumped in with a swathe of other industries – broadcast, events, circus – but it feels like the importance of live performance has slipped through the cracks. I think the population is starting to understand it a lot better now and starting to get their head around what's missing, but the people calling the shots are not there yet.

Hopefully, something will come soon and at a time when people can focus on it. We'll have lifted the lockdown for pubs and bars and the football will be playing, then hopefully it'll be our turn and we can say, "Look at this business, look at this industry who are suffering. Let's help them now." I've got absolute faith that there are people in our business who are representing us very well – whether it's producers or Equity – and some of the MPs are starting to represent us well too. There are also work groups, think tanks and with everything going on it can become a bit overwhelming. We have to be careful to time our banner-waving right or we'll get lost. It's just such a long wait.

The only thing that will drive the Government is money. If they think they will lose too much money, they will act. When they see how many people are involved in the arts and they think that things won't reopen until next year, they'll see the financial implications and the fact that an enormous part of the workforce will be unemployed. There won't be any jobs out there to give them either. We can't all just go out and start building houses and laying roads. That's not going to work is it?

It feels like an age ago that they closed the theatres. We'd just finished around four weeks of rehearsals and gone into tech at the Playhouse. We'd done four previews by the Saturday night and that performance was extraordinary. We finally felt like what we'd created on stage was really working with the audience. They were responding in a way that we could only have hoped for. It's a very special production: bringing Chekhov to a market who wouldn't normally be interested – that's the brilliance of Jamie Lloyd.

The way the company connected with each other and told the story together – that was the magic of it. They were so on point with their relationships: it was down to individual breaths or blinking and such small moments that were enormous on stage. You had to see it live: there was no way we could have filmed it and shown that level of performance. And telling a story in a way that it hasn't been told before.

We may hopefully come back in November. Who knows? They will have to re-invest and re-invent that and try and tell it again in the same way to an audience who hopefully really want to come and see it. ☞

# "You had to see it live: there was no way we could have filmed it and shown that level of performance."

## Rehearsals suspended
The auditorium - The Playhouse Theatre

During rehearsals we knew that Coronavirus was in play and it was already quite quiet when we came into the West End. By Saturday 14th it was really quiet. We celebrated on the Saturday with drinks and a pizza night after the show.

On the Monday morning we had understudy rehearsals scheduled. Phone calls started around 10am while I was on the train in. I feel like we were a little bit left out in the cold by the Government at that point. This was the moment when they should have been taking control. They should really have locked down and given strong, clear advice. All we were left with was NHS guidelines to self-isolate if you had symptoms. Also, there were only a couple of symptoms listed. I had to cancel a marketing meeting with Jamie Lloyd as it didn't feel appropriate, then phone calls started to come in from the technical departments with people saying they had flatmates who were symptomatic or they felt they were symptomatic. I spent my journey in firefighting, trying to cover the show. I knew that all the other company managers in the West End

were experiencing the same thing. We all knew that something was going to happen that week, it was just a question of when. I had another phone meeting when I arrived so I decided to walk from Victoria Station instead of going on the Underground. It was a beautiful day but there was just a handful of tourists. It was so surreal: everyone had cleared out.

From the point of arriving at the theatre I was firefighting again, this time with calls from the cast saying they had been feeling unwell. Minor symptoms the week before were now a massive concern. The pastoral care just didn't stop. I had one company member who was presenting with pretty strong symptoms so we decided they shouldn't come in. Thankfully, we had an understudy rehearsal but this is a tough script and it was their first chance to be on stage. The cast have multiple roles to learn. I was able to speak to the resident director and suggest that we focus on this specific character because there was every chance that the understudy was going to go on that evening. ☞

Whilst that rehearsal took place, I went to deal with Front of House matters. The week before, the show was sold out - it was a very popular show and company – but by the time we got to Saturday night our audiences were dropping. We had a returns queue outside for people wanting to see the show, but so many people just didn't turn up and didn't advise the theatre, so we still couldn't release the tickets. It was very clear that there was momentum from an audience perspective of not coming in because they didn't know whether it was safe. That Monday night was the first of our subsidised performances for young and disadvantaged audiences. The box office was saying that all the school groups were still intending to come in, so it was looking positive, but I didn't know how many people would actually turn up.

The staff were also swamped with enquiries about whether we were still on and trying to rebook people for about a week's time. The theatre management were trying to work out how to keep everything clean, punters were in wearing face masks and people were not wanting to sit next to patrons with coughs - it was all very surreal. By that stage, we were already wondering when a decision was going to be made about closures. We already knew about Broadway, so we were just waiting. We were very much praying we'd get through our press night. We had nothing to sell on at that point because we hadn't had press reviews.

We had a company meeting at 4pm which was going to be a notes session as part of our normal preview process. That turned into a conversation with the producer about how people were feeling and how we were addressing safety concerns including not allowing people backstage and supplying hand sanitiser. We reiterated that if the company had symptoms they didn't need to come in. The responsibility had been put onto the individual by the Government, and that was a very hard place to be. One of the company members had already decided that they weren't well enough to perform that evening, so we were able to confirm that the understudy who had been rehearsing earlier would be going on that night. That was a big thing for a company. ☞

## Shutters down
Front of House - The Playhouse Theatre

We had a break, then I went off to try and find something that could help boost the health of the company. There was no generalised testing – you could only get tested if you had been admitted to hospital. We had tried to go down the route of private testing, but it was £450 per kit - and they tended to be sold out. Instead I ordered vitamin B12 shots for the company to give their immune system a boost, so we had a nurse in a mask and gloves administering B12 around the building.

I also have responsibility for stage management within my role, so I was dealing with the technical departments and pre-setting for the show. As I was heading upstairs one of the company members came up to me and said, "have you heard what was on the news? There's been a press briefing." My heart sank. I just thought "What are we going to do?". You go into an emergency situation of trying to deal with the now and the present but you also start thinking about what the announcement meant for us as individuals and as an industry. As soon as the announcement telling audiences to stay away was made, I knew the gloves were off. There was no guideline that went along with it: it just felt like a throwaway comment in the middle of a press briefing. It validated everybody's concerns about whether to come in and see live theatre, without saying whether the theatres should close. As we tend to do in stage management or company management, we just said to the cast "You just carry on having your dinner and your vitamin shot, warm up, stay calm and we'll deal with it."

Then the phone calls to the producers started again in earnest. There was chaotic confusion around what was going on that evening on the one hand, whilst I tried to keep everything calm and normal backstage on the other. Around six, I got word via the theatre that all ATG venues were closing. That was the alarm bell. We now had something concrete to work with and my producer called me and asked me to meet him at the stage door, then we'd go and talk to the company and explain what's happened after warm-up.

We went up on stage and as soon as we got there we were mobbed. The cast were so on edge and overwhelmed by what they were feeling and the uncertainly, that it immediately came out: "We're closing the theatre". They had all been doing quite a high energy warm-up, so it wasn't an introverted moment when they found out. There were loud reactions, expressing the frustration that we were all feeling about the mixed messages from the government and every emotion possible. It would have been great if someone had had a camera. It was an absolutely surreal moment and so last-minute.

I was gutted for the cast, for the understudy who was supposed to be going on that night, for the company who we had told not to worry and promised that we'd give them guidelines, for the technical and creative teams who were hoping to get through to a press night. I felt like in that one moment, everything just slipped away – just disappeared.

Everyone was very emotional, then suddenly got very busy trying to work out what this all meant and what to do. We had to say, "There's nothing to do. We need you to all leave the building and go home." I then had to go around the building and speak to anyone who wasn't on stage and break the news. I told people not to leave any belongings that they might need tomorrow or next month, because I didn't know when we'd be back. We had to power everything down and make it all safe, clear the fridges and put dust covers over everything. ☞

"I felt like in that one moment everything just slipped away – just disappeared."

Going out front and seeing the theatre management having to deal with the audiences was really heart-breaking. The audience were arriving at the theatre only to be told that the whole West End was closing. It was a tragedy that they weren't given any notice. I mean, across the West End, even if the theatres had only been operating at 50% capacity, that would still have been over 20,000 people travelling in on public transport to be dumped in the West End with restaurants and theatres closing. Thank goodness they left the bars open that day.

Once we had cleared everyone out of the theatre we all went to the pub. I was the last one in there because I had to send an email out to everyone involved in the production to let them know that there wasn't going to be a show that evening. Sending that email felt like the nail in the coffin: that was it, the full stop. Thankfully we'd had the Saturday night which was a real celebration for us, but that night there was a sense of mourning. Everyone was trying to work out what they were going to do: do I stay in London? There was no lockdown yet, after all.

I think about all of these people who we were are about to undertake the next few months with. That relationship won't ever happen after all. Not with the people or the building. The theatres really become your home. Everyone's got their personal stuff there: in the women's dressing room they've got bean bags and in the men's they've got instruments. Being in the theatre industry is like being a member of a family. We're on lockdown away from the rest of our families and we can't go and see each other or meet the people we were about to get to know on new projects. So many of us are freelance or on short contracts and have friends in every corner of the West End. There are so many people I want to see and I can't think of how to do that. They only way is to come back to work.

That image shows our warm-up floor that was about to be rolled up ready for the performance. It was a very intense show and very relevant. It's about a whole group of people in isolation in one space and we illustrated that physically on stage so it's disappointing that we weren't able to present that to the public in an official opening. We were just stopped and our story remains untold.

My hope would be that the audiences come back with a new level of respect for live performance, in particular how important the interaction is between the performer on stage and the audience member in portraying emotion, and context for amazing words. Technically, we all consider ourselves to be creative in this environment: we are all in it together. It's a collaboration and I think we all feel the same level of involvement as the person who is standing on stage, as the person who is dressing, as the person on followspot - even those cleaning the theatre. We're all contributing to the same thing and I really hope that when the audiences come back – and they will – that they have a new level of understanding as to what it takes. The Jamie Lloyd Company were very much about bringing this piece to an audience who would never normally sit through Chekhov. Theatre is something we are privileged to have in all of our lives. ●

"My hope would be that the audiences come back with a new level of respect for live performance, in particular how important the interaction is between the performer on stage and the audience member..."

**Behind the iron**
The stage - The Playhouse Theatre

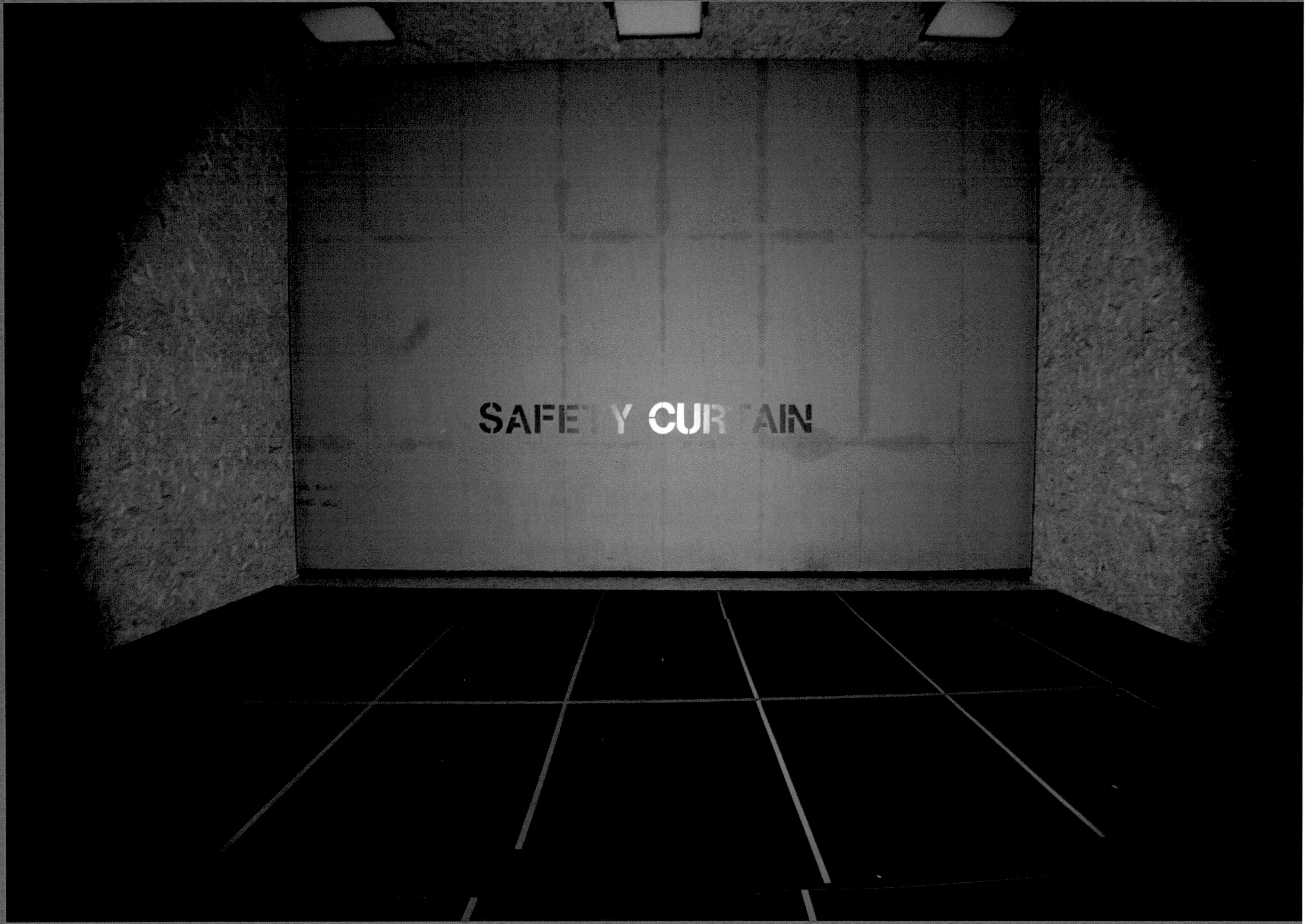
SAFETY CURTAIN

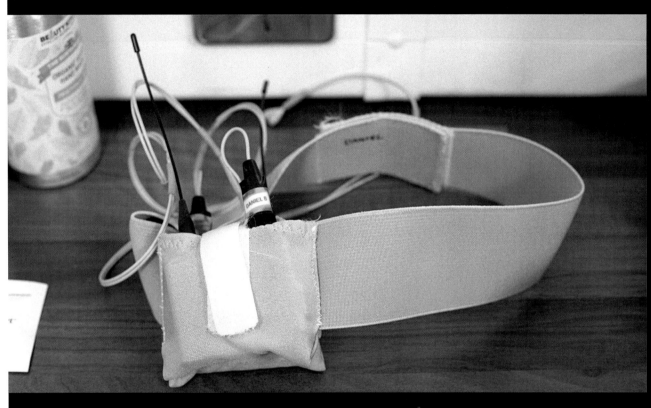

Left behind.

# 10

# Jen Raith

**Stage Manager** | *9 to 5: The Musical* | The Savoy Theatre, London

I'm at my mum's. It was the safest option. We've been up here since the week the theatres closed, around three days before the lockdown. I think for a lot of folk – especially those with family – they've gained time that they wouldn't normally have had. Mum's a nurse, and she's still working part-time at the hospital so she's been worried about patient contact. But she's been nowhere near COVID patients, because the hospital where she works is really well organised.

I went back to work when my daughter was ten weeks old. They managed to put me back in part-time, which was ideal. I think it's the future of things as well. Before this all kicked off, the management were talking to me about future projects and being part-time – letting somebody else start it and go through tech then coming in afterwards, even as an Assistant Stage Manager (I wouldn't have minded) – before my daughter, Phoebe, goes to preschool anyway. There are a lot of employers who can't see how it can work, especially as a Stage Manager, but thankfully the team were very willing to help out to get us back. Matt Cullum (General Manager, ATG), being a parent himself, wanted to be an advocate of the job share. That approach was gaining traction and I was enjoying going part-time and working out how to do it with Phoebe. That's all been quashed now though! It's too uncertain and it's just not worth the headache on top of trying to bring up a little one. 🏳

**A prop sandwich on stage**
The Savoy Theatre

"I went back to work when my daughter was ten weeks old. They managed to put me back in part-time, which was ideal. I think it's the future of things as well."

# "It's an odd situation that none of us will ever, ever be in again. It's going to be so hard to explain to people. Not even in World War II did all the theatres shut down."

It's been lovely being a full-time mum. I'm not going to complain. She's a lovely baby – so chilled out. Because we're not at any toddler groups I have been putting on programs from the BBC, so she can see the other babies. You know, dealing with a baby is a lot easier than dealing with actors, that's for sure.

We're lucky because Martin's a 'doer'. He was with FOYS up at *Harry Potter* on the Monday when we were sent home and by Wednesday evening he had a new job. He ended up working for DPD doing overnight shifts for about three months. It sent him loopy but he just had to find work. He's been picking up odds and sods like everyone else at the moment to keep money coming in, so he stayed in London and we haven't seen him for four months. Four months in a baby's life is big, you know. She was seven months when we left and now she's nearly a year old. We video call every day, but you can't get a sense of what she's like now physically. We're going back down south on Thursday and he's going to see a huge change in her – all these steps that she's taken since she's been up here, you know – crawling, all these words, and she's starting to toddle now. It was the most sensible thing to do though.

Nicola Sturgeon has been playing it sensibly safe and we've felt very secure up here. I think it would have been a very different story staying down south with Martin going to work every day during the spike, not knowing who he's coming into contact with. I'd be very different person. We're still wearing our masks and gloves, but I think I would be more neurotic about it if I'd been at home in London.

We'd gone in to work and set up the show on the Monday and we were going about our business as normal. We were getting information on the news but we didn't really realise the extent of it. They had said it was a bit like SARS and it might just disappear; then it was ramping up and getting more serious in Italy. There had been word that London might lock down, but again there was nothing on the news, nothing from the Government to say this was about to happen. We were hearing through the afternoon that folk were being told not to go in to work. Cameron Mackintosh shut *Hamilton* in the afternoon and Nica Burns followed suit. *Harry Potter* was another one – Sonia Friedman had pulled shows on Broadway the week before so she was prepared. ☞

## Prop clipboards
The Savoy Theatre

At five o'clock, Sarah [Whalley, Company Manager] came down and said "Matt's on his way down. I think we're about to get some news". We knew what that meant, but the cast were thinking, "Oh my God, we're shutting early!" because usually when the general manager makes an announcement that's what it is. Matt talked for about ten minutes, explaining the discussions with producers and Westminster. He told us that due to circumstances we couldn't let audiences in and they wanted to make sure that we were safe. At that point he didn't have any more information – not even about the rest of the week – and he said they would be in touch.

Within the hour, the iron had dropped and everybody went outside and headed to the pub. We only went for a couple, because all of a sudden there was this reality hit - it was actually getting serious. We'd watched it on the news and knew it was severe, but we didn't know how severe. Sitting and talking over that pint, it suddenly hit home that it was bigger than we had all expected. I had all the ASMs with me and they asked what I thought was going to happen. My opinion at that point (and it turned out to be correct) was that I could imagine the producers being quite frightened because they'd not been told by the Government to shut down and they wouldn't know whether or not the insurances would cover them. I did say at this point I thought it would be a couple of months. The fear suddenly set in. We all had the same question: what's going to happen next?

"I don't reckon I will go back to doing what I did before, not right now. I don't want the uncertainty as a freelancer. I've always felt lucky doing what I do – I've always gone from job to job and I've met some amazing people… but I just need to have a break with all of this going on."

### Interconnected economies

Mr. Fogg's Pub, St. Martin's Lane

We kept in touch over the coming days. I went in on the Wednesday to do a tidy up of batteries and make it safe, but there were minimal folk in. And coming in from Beckenham – you know what it's like in the centre of London at six in the morning on a Sunday: it's dead. That's what it was like in the middle of the week at ten o'clock on a Wednesday. It was bizarre – like *28 Days Later*. I had to walk over Waterloo Bridge that day and it was deserted. Really odd. There was nobody on the train, nobody on the Tube. That was my weird moment in all of this. It was abandonment, like everybody had just jumped away. I was away by one o'clock in the afternoon. I said goodbye to everybody and then just had to go with the flow.

I don't reckon I will go back to doing what I did before, not right now. I don't want the uncertainty as a freelancer. I've always felt lucky doing what I do – I've had no gaps: I've always gone from job to job and I've met some amazing people – but the kind of things we can deal with on our own without family involved, I can't deal with any more with my daughter. I just need to have a break with all of this going on. In a weird way it's come at a good time in her life: she's a baby, we're not having to worry about schools. In a strange way the universe has worked in our favour because we can take a step back and use this time for family. And that's the way it should be.

It's an odd situation that none of us will ever, ever be in again. Not even in World War II did all the theatres shut down. That's bonkers. We're not the only industry that's been affected but we're so lucky that as a community in theatre we band together so well. Look at what we've managed to do: we've made it onto the news, the unions have been on. There are thousands of people in the UK who don't have that camaraderie so we're very lucky to have each other.

With any luck, the theatre world will come back bigger and stronger, because we have the opportunity to start from the ground up. I'd rather come back into an industry at a level where everybody's comfortable and you're not fighting for the jobs. My CV's not going anywhere. I'll just take everybody for pints. That's how my career started - by taking everybody for a pint, so I'll just carry on doing that! ●

A glimpse
at the
bigger
picture.

Backstage at the
Union Theatre
Photographed by Ben Bull

The Set of *Harry Potter*
under wraps at
The Palace Theatre
Photographed by James Humby

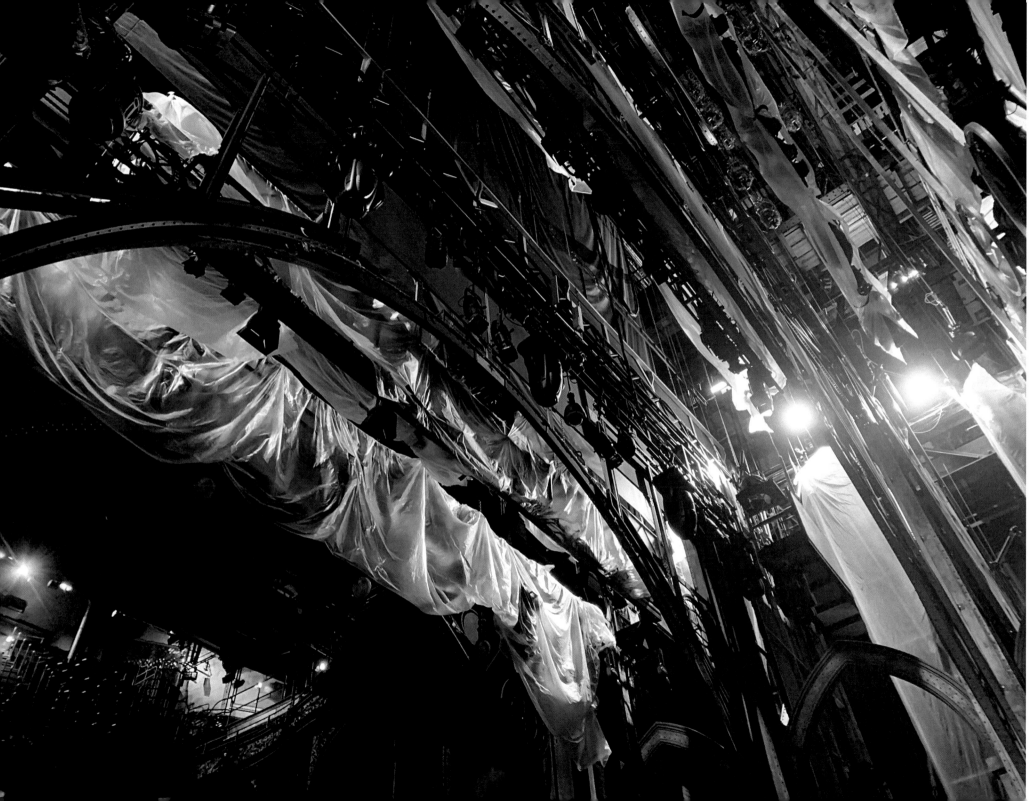

# II

# Cameron Slater

Photographer | *Directors' Office Administrator* | The Royal National Theatre

I have been taking photographs semi-professionally for about fourteen years and a lot of the work I have done has been for the National Theatre. I have worked there as an employee for the same amount of time too. I started in the Development Department taking photos for their big events and galas and then I worked at the box office whilst I was still an actor. When I started as a head-shot photographer, the NT kindly let me use their spaces and terraces. The light bounces off the concrete delightfully.

For the past three years I have worked full-time assisting the Joint Chief Executives as part of the NT's Directors Office team, so my photography activity has dwindled a bit. I think when I retired from being an actor it really took me by surprise how much acting was something that I held so much as part of my identity. Although it was completely the right decision, I did feel quite adrift. I'm just really happy that I found a job that I love as much as acting, even if I'm surprised that it involves sitting at a desk nine-to-five in front of spreadsheets and emails! I have always loved the National, so it feels like a real privilege to help the people who are making the things I love happen. ☞

**A ghost ship**
The National Theatre
© *Cameron Slater*

> "It was as if somebody had just said 'Out, now', and people had left not knowing that they wouldn't be coming back."

It's tricky at the moment of course. I am on furlough. As a theatre we're facing financial difficulties due to the closure. The staff have all taken a voluntary 20% pay cut and unfortunately the whole organisation is in the middle of a redundancy process, like many theatres across the UK, so everything is really quite grim right now.

In the week before the lockdown was announced, we were getting prepared and were all being told how to set up from home. My main memory of that week was from the Monday. We only had one show on that evening, *The Visit*, and I remember Rufus [Norris] had to go and speak to the company. *The Visit* had a huge cast and they were so keen to perform to the audience still: it was amazing. He had to talk it through with them and they eventually made the difficult decision to cancel the show on that day. I think there was only one performance in the entire country that went ahead that night, so we were by no means the only ones not to perform.

When I went into the office afterwards, I suddenly felt it was getting real. I took a box of my things home a couple of days later and ordered a new desk, because I thought, "If I'm going to be sitting here for a bit, I want to be comfortable." I haven't moved since! The geography of it is so weird. I take for granted how much my desk in the office allowed me to receive information by just sitting there and now I'm completely out of the loop. We do all stay in touch quite a bit, which is lovely.

After about three weeks of furlough, my colleague and I were asked to go in to sort through the sacks of post that had been accumulating while we were closed. On the second day I took my camera in as I thought this would be quite a good opportunity. When I opened my laptop, I found an email from the head of the NT Archive asking if at some point I would be prepared to go in and take some photos, so it was a really happy accident that I had! It was a real privilege to do it. I don't think I will forget it in a hurry.

## Silent

The National Theatre
© *Cameron Slater*

We were sorting the post in one of the rehearsal rooms. That in itself felt new – it isn't my environment any more – and it was like Pompeii: there were cups of tea, abandoned actors' trainers, scripts next to chairs. It was as if somebody had just said "Out, now!" and people had left not knowing that they wouldn't be coming back. That was quite eerie.

Going back to our office was odd because it had only been about a month. It felt quite ghostly at first, then remarkably, after about forty-five minutes it felt no different at all – back to usual at my usual desk.

The one thing that the photos could never capture is how silent it was. Usually there is a hubbub of audiences and noise from offices, but I'd just turned a corner to come down a corridor and you could hear the tiny click of the movement sensor activating the light. At night you might have expected that silence, but this was during the day.

I was working on admin during the day, so it was only around quarter to seven that I got to go out with my camera. When I went Front of House, it really hit home. I had a realisation that at that time on a Friday night that building was usually at its peak of vibrancy, but it was like a ghost ship. The evening sun was pouring in. I completely lucked out with the light. Had I taken a lunch break it would have been completely different, I think.

It's such a beast of a building – this hulking concrete heaviness – it was like it was sitting there having a really deep sleep. I was surprised how un-eerie I found it: I wasn't spooked at any point. I thought I would be – walking around a dark theatre – but it was one of the most secure feelings: no dark corners were a threat. In the moment it just felt really, really comforting - like the building was too big and too important for anything to really let it die. I felt its strength was apparent and quite reassuring. It was really lovely. And it was beautiful. Over the years I have really fallen in love with the architecture.

"The one thing that the photos could never capture is how silent it was. It's such a beast of a building – this hulking concrete heaviness – it was like it was sitting there having a really deep sleep."

On a personal level, I hope that I get to go back. I think it's very much at the front of mine and a lot of my colleagues' minds. Regardless of where my position might fall, I think this is an opportunity for the industry to have a moment of self-reflection. There is a lot that's happening aside from the troubles we're experiencing. With George Floyd and the Black Lives Matter movement there is a mirror being held up to all of us and making us think about the way we see ourselves, and I think that self-reflection should continue and spread across the industry. It's maybe a moment to press the reset button.

Then again, part of me would just love to go back to the certainty of February. I think I am still mourning the shows we were about to open and the programming we were about to announce. Because I've been on furlough I have not quite got my head around the fact that we'll have to wait much longer to see so much of the work we were gearing up to do.

I think there are some very exciting things about the situation too – we work with creative people and they are thinking creatively about what can happen and what we can do, not just by way of an artistic response but also what can we do that is going to be of help, financially. Even that is still a creative thought process and I'm excited to see how that could all play out. I'm desperate to be a part of helping the National Theatre make that work. I'm confident it will happen somehow and if there is any part I can play in rising from the ashes, I'd love to help.

A lot of people across all sectors are having to think about things they have never had to think about before – problems they would never have imagined having to navigate – in government too. None of us has done this before.

I do have faith in our industry's leaders to really be creative and strong and to fight. I know that Rufus and Lisa have just not stopped. I know they have been pulling all-nighters on occasions and given that we have no shows going on, I don't know how they are managing! I feel incredibly reassured that they are doing it. The same goes for all the leaders – Sonia [Friedman], Nica [Burns] Mike Longhurst, Vicki Featherstone – everybody is just on fire. I find them all really inspiring. Also, so many people in the industry are freelancers and by the nature of that career choice have had to have resilience. Resourcefulness is a way of life for them and it makes me feel like we're in safe hands. Looking ahead to the future, there are just so many unknowns, but I expect to be inspired by lots of people. ●

**Evening light**
The National Theatre
*© Cameron Slater*

"I think there are some very exciting things about the situation too – we work with creative people and they are thinking creatively about what can happen and what we can do, not just by way of an artistic response, but also what can we do that is going to be of help, financially."

Waitin

The National

# 12 My story

## Nina Dunn Author & Photographer

Video & Projection Designer | *City of Angels* | The Garrick Theatre, London

"I had seen the events industry slowly cancel numerous fixtures over the weeks before and now it was our turn. I let the tears flow as I started to process it all."

I was at the Garrick, preparing to lock the show ahead of press night the following week. Like many of my interviewees I knew we were on a timeline to closure. From the Thursday before the theatres closed, each time I took my seat for a performance I had a feeling that it might be the last.

I had started to become concerned about the risks I might pose to my asthmatic daughter by bringing COVID back home from the theatre. My programmer was also asthmatic, so we had already taken to doing notes with him upstairs in the control area on headphones that linked down to me in the auditorium below in an attempt to protect him.

On the Saturday before the closures, I had been asked by the director and producers to record the performance for reference purposes as my department had the required equipment on-site. By the Monday I definitely felt like we shouldn't be there still and so did many of the cast, but we wanted to last out one more day and invite reviewers in early so that at least we'd have a press night of sorts. While we were having a company meeting with the theatre owner, Nica Burns, to discuss how to proceed, the announcement from Boris was broadcast and the sound team fed it out into the auditorium via the house P.A.. The cast and crew all just sat grimly listening, then we all broke out into union groups to discuss what to do next. The director, Josie Rourke, felt that the announcement was very unclear so she and Nica consulted with SOLT (The Society of London Theatres) before subsequently officially calling the show off.

Nica kindly offered us all a farewell drink in the bar. It was really a unique atmosphere – a moment to remember. Cast members from *Everybody's Talking About Jamie* joined us still wearing full drag make up ready for the evening's performance. There were some people already wearing gloves and masks whilst others were freely hugging and consoling each other. We all speculated about the future. I remember one crew member telling me she had just £500 in the bank and didn't know how she was going to survive.

I actually felt relieved that I would get some time to spend at home with the kids. I was exhausted. Unless you work in theatre, I don't think you can really grasp how hard a tech week can be. You have to put all the technical elements of the show together in a very limited time frame because it's incredibly

### The Garrick Theatre

The view from the technical gallery
On stage during the announcement
Locked gates

expensive to have a theatre closed to audiences. Everyone involved has to work at top capacity to feed the beast – the story, the show – against a very hard and fast deadline – 1,000 audience members arriving to see what you have created. You work long days and live off the adrenaline. I happened to be logging my time for a survey on designers' wages at the time and it had showed that my average tech week ran to more than ninety hours. After a jam-packed start to the year, I was due to go into development with new shows once *City of Angels* had opened and then off to Australia with a touring production, so I was psychologically prepared for a change of pace and activity. I don't think the reality of it hit me until later: I never thought it would be such a full stop.

When I left the theatre, I took a taxi to the station with my equipment and headed back to Brighton. I remember thinking that by taking the freelance career path you should avoid ever experiencing that crashing moment of coming home to announce to your family that you have lost your job. Usually contracts are of a limited duration and there are always other opportunities out there, both nationally and internationally, but in this instance our whole industry had collapsed overnight. The full weight of this hit me. I had seen the events

industry slowly cancel numerous fixtures over the weeks before and now it was our turn. I let the tears flow as I started to process it all.

I tried not to think about the fact that after eight years of working to break through in the West End I was set to have three shows running simultaneously this spring for a short time, which crucially also meant that the financial gains would finally justify the hard work and time away from my family too. I tried not to think how I had fought to stay in the industry after becoming a mother and through bringing up two girls against what sometimes seemed like all odds. I tried not to believe that all was lost.

This was a week before the official lockdown was enforced. My husband, Tom, suggested I should go shopping to stock up during the daytime so that I could avoid the crowds but, in my mind, I was thinking "Can I even spend money? Perhaps I should stick to doing an inventory of the larder". There had been no government announcements suggesting income support at all and I had no idea when I would ever be paid again. The population at large seemed to be on a different trajectory to those who had been ejected from their jobs in the theatre: still cramming into sweaty coffee shops and heading in to work. ☞

# "We just need a leg up. Then watch us fly."

**9 to 5: a standing ovation**
The Savoy Theatre
© Pamela Raith

All the mums who aren't used to seeing me at the school and nursery gates were saying, "Oh you're back!" and I felt like shouting, "Don't you realise? I'm not just back from the latest show. My entire industry has collapsed! Why isn't the county in lockdown? The sooner we go in the sooner we can come out!".

I hurriedly gathered essentials from my studio and set up to work from home but I struggled to be motivated – one by one, each of the shows that I had lined up for rest of the year slowly died a death. It was as if on 16th March they had all been given a terminal diagnosis then proceeded to go through various stages of illness and remission (threat of cancellation then postponement) before - by and large – succumbing to the terminal prognosis of cancellation.

I was also deathly exhausted. I am used to this state of being following an intensive tech – I call it 'show lag' because the feeling resembles jet lag so closely. A heavy lethargy sets in and the need to nap several times each day is desperate and urgent, but after three days it was not improving. It was only when I couldn't for the life of me smell the lilies I received as a Mother's Day present that I realised that I had this new symptom that was being discussed – the loss of smell and taste – and that I had contracted Coronavirius.

Soon after, we lost a dear family member and with that, the world had changed beyond all recognition. Everything was brought into sharp perspective.

Like so many people, lockdown has meant adjusting to a completely different pace and structure to life. I have spent a lot more time with the kids, which has been welcome, but like most parents I have struggled with home schooling. Most of us are not teachers by nature or profession, especially not ones who can span two or more entirely different year groups and even if regular work had dried up, there was a great deal of admin to do around mothballing my business.

I do teach at undergraduate level so the effort to move classes at RADA online was all-consuming in the weeks ahead of term starting again and all the while I had to remain optimistic that this teaching would not be in vain. But even once the health emergency seemed to be under control and we were looking towards lifting the lockdown, the Government seemed to refuse to be able to say the word 'theatre' in their briefings and it started to feel like conscious neglect.

I also struggled with having no creative outlet. Like so many other freelance individuals, I don't say, "I work at" I say, "I AM". I have been described as a prolific maker and it felt as if I had lost a large part of my being. Slowly as I recovered from the shock of the first few weeks, I started to make again and with it to heal. My first few projects were heavily orientated towards involving the children, like projection-mapping a Lego hospital they built. I started to thrive on conversations with other creatives, even if the projects we conjured up were hypothetical. Then one day, I started to wonder what the theatres were like inside after being left so suddenly and for so long and so *The Dark Theatres Project* was born.

If some good has come out of this extended closure, at least there is a greater awareness of the social and financial contribution that our industry makes to the wider community and economy. We have been forced to justify our existence in undeniable facts and figures. As painful as it was to answer so very many questionnaires and continually evaluate the vast extent to which our livelihoods have been lost, at least we now have this proof. The Government also now better understands the genetic make-up of the theatre community and importantly how much of it relies on a freelance workforce. We have seen this group of highly skilled freelance specialists – artists, producers and technicians alike – all band together to stand up for the industry we love in the face of a government which doesn't seem to understand any career path that deviates from the norm.

In the time of such a life-changing global crisis, artists have once again become activists – for community, justice, diversity – and rightly so. We should be a mirror to society and beg questions of humanity that need debate. I hope we re-emerge stronger and more diverse. If any group of people can, it's us; but after years of funding being systematically stripped away from the Arts while society and the Government continues to reap the benefits, we just need a leg up. Then watch us fly. ●

This book is being sold to raise funds for four charities that help theatre workers and buildings in crisis.

# About the charities

Backup | The Theatrical Guild | The Theatres Trust | Acting For Others

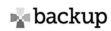

**Backup** is the Technical Entertainment Charity. It provides financial support to industry technical professionals working in live events, theatre, TV and film. If you or a family member are seriously ill or suffering from an accident and needing support or if there is someone you know who needs help, Backup can offer support and help to get you back on your feet.

**The Theatrical Guild** is a UK charity for backstage and front of house workers, with over 125 years' experience of helping people. It provides practical help from welfare and debt advice to financial support and counselling.

**The Theatres Trust** is the national advisory public body for theatres. If you are looking to build a new theatre, are an existing theatre in need of advice or funding, or are working to bring a theatre back to life, it has expert advice and resources to help.

**Acting For Others** was founded in the 1960s when Laurence Olivier, together with Noël Coward and Richard Attenborough, had the idea of promoting a single annual fund-raising event for all theatrical charities. It now provides financial and emotional support to all theatre workers in times of need through its 14 member charities.

## Thank you.

All of the images featured in this book and more are available as C-Type archive prints. Discover more at **www.darktheatresproject.org**